Martin Kramer, *University of California, Berkeley*
EDITOR-IN-CHIEF

Financial Management: Progress and Challenges

William E. Vandament
Northern Michigan University

Dennis P. Jones
*National Center for Higher Education
Management Systems*

EDITORS

Number 83, Fall 1993

JOSSEY-BASS PUBLISHERS
San Francisco

FINANCIAL MANAGEMENT: PROGRESS AND CHALLENGES
William E. Vandament, Dennis P. Jones (eds.)
New Directions for Higher Education, no. 83
Volume XXI, Number 3
Martin Kramer, Editor-in-Chief

Microfilm copies of issues and articles are available in 16mm and 35mm, as well as microfiche in 105mm, through University Microfilms Inc., 300 North Zeeb Road, Ann Arbor, Michigan 48106-1346.

LC 85-644752   ISSN 0271-0560   ISBN 1-55542-722-7

NEW DIRECTIONS FOR HIGHER EDUCATION is part of The Jossey-Bass Higher and Adult Education Series and is published quarterly by Jossey-Bass Inc., Publishers, 350 Sansome Street, San Francisco, California 94104-1310 (publication number USPS 990-880). Second-class postage paid at San Francisco, California, and at additional mailing offices. POSTMASTER: Send address changes to New Directions for Higher Education, Jossey-Bass Inc., Publishers, 350 Sansome Street, San Francisco, California 94104-1310.

SUBSCRIPTIONS for 1993 cost $47.00 for individuals and $62.00 for institutions, agencies, and libraries.

EDITORIAL CORRESPONDENCE should be sent to the Editor-in-Chief, Martin Kramer, 2807 Shasta Road, Berkeley, California 94708.

Cover photograph and random dot by Richard Blair/Color & Light © 1990.

Manufactured in the United States of America. Nearly all Jossey-Bass books, jackets, and periodicals are printed on recycled paper that contains at least 50 percent recycled waste, including 10 percent postconsumer waste. Many of our materials are also printed with vegetable-based ink; during the printing process these inks emit fewer volatile organic compounds (VOCs) than petroleum-based inks. VOCs contribute to the formation of smog.

CONTENTS

EDITORS' NOTES   1
William E. Vandament, Dennis P. Jones

1. Strategic Budgeting   5
Dennis P. Jones
Institutional assets are protected best when the administration actively
defines the budgeting strategy.

2. The Cost of General Education   17
Robert P. Lisensky
Arts and science departments can use general education programs to
generate resources that pay for inefficient major programs.

3. Activity-Based Costing: A Cost Management Tool   27
Frederick J. Turk
Activities that indirectly support other activities are seldom analyzed to
reveal the actual basis of overhead costs.

4. Strategic Restructuring: A Case Study   35
James A. Hyatt
Effective strategies for dealing with financial challenges entail rethinking
sources of funding for programs as well as establishing priorities for
activities.

5. An Analysis of Oregon State University's   43
Total Quality Management Pilot Program
L. Edwin Coate
A team approach can be an effective way to improve services by placing more
power in the hands of those providing them.

6. Multidimensional Analyses and Cost-Revenue Relationships   63
William E. Vandament
Increasingly sophisticated analyses of costs and revenues have contributed
to more effective financial management in U.S. higher education.

INDEX   75

EDITORS' NOTES

Financial management in American higher education has been the focus of much attention since the mid 1960s. It was during that time that the development of computer information systems made more information available to managers, and various states were confronted with finding appropriate funding levels for growing colleges and universities. Many states attempted to develop funding formulas that took into account the different financial needs of programs in various disciplines and the differences in cost that were incurred at various levels of postsecondary education. The Western Interstate Commission for Higher Education (WICHE) attempted to fill an information void by developing methods to analyze costs by discipline and level of instruction for purposes of comparison among institutions. This activity to develop a national network for the comparison of program costs immediately caught the attention of the National Association of College and University Business Officers. That organization then formed a financial management committee, known unofficially as the "WICHE Watchers," whose activities subsequently have paralleled the development of more sophisticated financial management in higher education.

This volume, *Financial Management: Progress and Challenges,* contains a compendium of observations and case studies by several observers, both daily practitioners in universities and others who serve in a consulting role, on topics that they deem important in financial management today. The topics run the gamut from relatively abstract concepts to detailed descriptions of the development and implementation of quality-management systems.

In Chapter One, Dennis P. Jones criticizes a "fixation on distribution of financial resources as the centerpiece of budgetary decision making." He notes that the typical planning process assumes that no change in services is best for the institution and largely attributes that inertia to the fact that most budgeting is centered in the institutional units, with only minimal guidance from the central administrations of colleges and universities. Making the point that such budgeting is likely to lead to a focus on consumption rather than investment for the future, he enumerates the various kinds of intangible assets that tend to be ignored because they are always somebody else's responsibility. These intangible assets include the quality and continued professional development of faculty and staff and the perceptions of the institution's quality and role on the part of the public and other consumers.

In Chapter Two, Robert P. Lisensky tackles what he perceives as waste and lack of direction in general education programs. Noting that in many institutions there are numbers of underutilized arts and science courses, he observes with some irony that the primary criteria used for hiring and retaining faculty are largely irrelevant to the tasks that these individuals are required to perform. In short, he notes that many faculty in the traditional arts and sciences disciplines have little interest in, or ability to teach, elementary courses to nonmajors and suggests as an alternative the effective integration of general education programs into those of the majors, particularly the professional program majors.

In Chapter Three, Frederick J. Turk advances the concept of activity-based costing, with a major focus on the overhead costs of running an institution. Noting that "institutions are captives of their financial accounting systems," he points out that these systems provide little information about factors that are actually consuming resources. He advocates a detailed activity analysis of service operations to determine in just which activities major expenditures are being made. He observes that overhead costs of programs are typically allocated by means of some rough proxy such as number of faculty or course enrollments rather than the actual processes used to support the programs. He believes that supporting operations such as registration, admission, financial aid, and financial administration can be conducted more efficiently through activity reengineering.

In Chapter Four, James A. Hyatt presents a case study of strategic restructuring processes at the University of Maryland at College Park. These activities represent a university's attempt to establish mission priorities first and then to undertake detailed review of not only the institution's expenditures but also the manner in which it generates its revenue. In part, the University of Maryland at College Park attempted to make certain that all services were generating appropriate revenues so that subsidies from the institution's unrestricted general funds could be reduced. While emphasizing the reallocation of existing funds to meet high priorities, the university also recognized the need for future monitoring and regularly scheduled analyses to ensure that "the sources of revenue are appropriate to the programs or services provided."

In Chapter Five, L. Edwin Coate provides examples of the several areas subjected to Total Quality Management (TQM) efforts at Oregon State University. Many issues were addressed, including reduction of time taken to complete remodeling processes, decreased errors in departmental journal vouchers, reduction of time expended in processing grant and contract documents, and reduction of response time to requests for public safety services. Coate notes that the users, or "customers," of various services were satisfied with the resulting improvements and that employee morale was improved by the process because it removed stumbling blocks to getting things done and increased employees' involvement in their jobs. Coate also noted, however, that the TQM process can be time-consuming and that it is important, therefore, either to relax production requirements during such studies or to conduct them when the volume of activities is low.

Finally, in Chapter Six, William E. Vandament leads the reader through the development of analytical tools in the financial management of higher education institutions. Perhaps optimistically, he states that many institutions are operating at a more sophisticated management level than previously. He notes the increased emphasis on basic cost-revenue relationships, in contrast to earlier practices that emphasized costs almost to the exclusion of concerns about the generation of revenue. He applauds the more active participation of higher education managers in cash management programs and the greater sophistication in investment of one-time funds to achieve savings on a year-to-year basis. From the perspective of this twenty-five year review, he believes that much progress in university financial management has occurred.

William E. Vandament
Dennis P. Jones
Editors

WILLIAM E. VANDAMENT is president and professor of psychology at Northern Michigan University, Marquette.

DENNIS P. JONES is president of the National Center for Higher Education Management Systems, Boulder, Colorado.

Institutional assets are protected best when the central administration provides clear direction.

Strategic Budgeting

Dennis P. Jones

The most commonly held perspective on budgeting in American higher education is likely that expressed by Caruthers and Orwig (1979, p. 1): "The budget is an instrument that enables the allocation of resources from one organizational unit to another, whether it be from a department to a faculty member, from a college to a department, from a university to a college, or from a funder to the university." This definition brings the distributional function of the budget to the forefront; it describes budgeting as a process unfettered by linkages to plans and priorities. Jones (1984, p. 13), however, emphasized this linkage, noting that "a budget's primary function is to span the distance between intention and action. It is the device by which [an organization] carries out its plans and by which it signals its priorities."

A synthesis of these two, and other, generally similar, definitions yields the conclusion that budgeting is a process of *making decisions that distribute resources to enable action.* Disassembling this composite definition and inspecting the components more closely can be instructive. First, the definition calls attention to the obvious but often overlooked fact that a budget represents a collection of decisions. As such, various approaches to budgeting are best understood by focusing on the kinds of decisions required in the process rather than on the various processes by which those decisions are achieved. Second, the definition serves to reinforce the notion that the purpose of the budget is to implement the institution's plans; the budget is a major (but not the only) tool for ensuring that institutional goals are pursued and, in the end, achieved.

On a conceptual level, there is seldom serious disagreement with these two points, once articulated and considered. Further, the simple phrase that the budget distributes resources is likely unquestioned as an expression of the essence of what budgeting is about. The overriding concern of most participants in the budgeting process is "Who gets how much?"—a question that reveals a fixation on distribution of financial resources as the centerpiece of budgetary decision making. The central thesis of this chapter is that this focus is entirely too narrow if the intent of the budget is to implement an institution's *strategic* plan. The development of an accompanying strategic budget requires a mechanism that places a series of decisions about the productive assets of the enterprise at the heart of the process.

Importance of Strategic Budgeting

Experience reveals that the budgeting exercise at many institutions starts and stops with the acquisition and allocation of financial resources. The budget process revolves around the tasks of estimating revenue changes and allocating increases (and, in some case, decreases) among the operating units of the institution. To the extent that budget guidelines are prepared centrally, they tend to include estimates of enrollment and revenue changes and to establish limits on price increases that will be allowed in major areas. The size of the salary increases for faculty tends to capture the greatest attention in such guidelines, but it is very common for the guidelines also to establish limits on allowable budgetary increases in such areas as travel, supplies, and equipment. The initial determination of salary increases frequently reflects consideration of salary levels at comparable institutions; targeted levels in other areas typically reflect inflationary changes in the prices of goods and services.

The guidelines may also establish overall limits for the various functional units of the institution: academic affairs, business affairs, student services, and so on. Within the guidelines, departments are asked to submit budget requests. Most such processes also allow special requests for additions to the departments' base budgets—the addition of faculty, for example—or for one-time expenditures for equipment or other items. Such requests are usually dealt with at the midmanagement or vice presidential level, with the basis of judgment most frequently being changes in workload (student demand for courses, larger physical plant to clean, and so on). In almost all cases, the initiative for identifying needs must come from unit heads; institution-level administrators enter the decision-making process when it becomes necessary to choose among competing requests.

This very common approach to budgeting has two noteworthy characteristics. First, it serves to constrain the domain of decisions made within the budget formulation process. The focus of decision making is on the prices that the institution is willing (or required) to pay to maintain the status quo. Fundamental questions about the quantity, quality, mix, and utilization of assets are addressed only when it becomes clear that inaction is no longer an option. Absent that kind of pressure, such questions are answered by assuming that "no change" best serves the needs of the institution.

Second, the approach is fundamentally unit-centered rather than institution-centered, a reflection of the fact that institutionwide administrators are basically reactive rather than proactive participants in the process. As a consequence, some of the core obligations of institutional administrators—to maintain, enhance, and shape the assets and the capacity of the institution as a whole—become subordinated to the sum of the decisions made at the unit level. This delegation of decision authority is unlikely to result in adequate investments in those assets that are everybody's and yet nobody's, such as buildings, certain equipment, and library books. This delegation of authority is also unlikely to result in necessary redistribution of assets, for example, eliminating some administrators and replacing them with faculty or other categories of personnel. When such trade-offs do occur, it is usually because competing alternatives are brought to senior administrators sitting as a court of last resort. But by the time institution-level administrators are confronted with these choices, it is likely that decision makers at lower levels have foreclosed options that would have better served institutional purposes (or that the options that would have better served the institution were never considered).

This approach also ensures that the budgetary levers that institutional leaders can use to change the institution are very short. They consist largely of marginal (incentive or categorical) funds set aside for this express purpose. The possibilities of change are enhanced when assumptions about the asset base of the institution are challenged and changes are made as opportunities allow.

These characteristics make approaches that embody them poor mechanisms for carrying out an institution's strategic plan. When planning is conducted at the strategic (institutional) level and budgeting is centered at the operational (unit) level, the linkages necessary to move an institution in the directions identified in the plan become fragile at best. There is a need for strategic budgeting as well as strategic planning, for an approach to budgeting that reflects an institutionwide perspective on resource allocation, that focuses on the basic asset structure of the institution rather than on the prices of those assets, and that puts central administrators in a proactive rather than a reactive role in this process.

The purpose of this chapter is to propose an approach to strategic budgeting that places decisions about the acquisition, maintenance, and utilization of institutional assets at the center of the budget process. The characteristics of assets that represent decision points in the budget process are examined, and the trade-offs among these decisions are discussed. In addition, the implications of this approach for the procedures of the budget process and for the roles of institutional administrators in the process are presented.

Basic Concepts of Strategic Budgeting

True consumables—payments for insurance, utilities, travel, and expendable office and laboratory supplies—represent a relatively small portion of an institution's budget. At most institutions, the proportion is less than a quarter. Payments for purchased services, particularly the services of part-time faculty, may drive this proportion higher. At the extreme, however, such payments seldom represent more than 30 to 40 percent. The rest of the budget comprises payments made to create or maintain the institution's assets, those tangible things and intangible rights that constitute the valued resources of the enterprise.

Although most of an institution's budget reflects the costs associated with creating and maintaining various kinds of assets (faculty and staff, equipment, physical plant, library and numerous collections, curricula, and such intangible assets as reputation or image), a relatively small portion of the energy that goes into budgeting is directed to decisions about the assets. Instead, attention centers on the financial resources that the institution chooses to invest in these assets on an annual basis. Thus, attention is focused on planned expenditures for faculty salaries rather than on the size and nature of the faculty desired by the institution, on expenditures for library collections rather than on the size and nature of the collection appropriate for the institution, and on the amount of money that can be squeezed out for curriculum development rather than on the philosophy of the institution regarding curriculum review and renewal. By emphasizing the financial resource equivalents of the asset structure in the budget decision-making process, institutional administrators essentially abdicate their responsibility to maintain and enhance the institution's asset base. In accounting terms, they become fixated on the revenue and expenditure statement to the detriment of a concern with the institution's balance sheet, which focuses on its assets and its net worth.

A very subtle consequence of a budgetary process that puts a premium on decisions about the distribution of financial resources is the delegation of many of an institution's strategic decisions to a managerial group that has neither an institutionwide perspective nor an incentive to act in the best interests of the institution as a whole. Deans, directors, and department chairs can and should be expected to pursue the best interests of their respective units. Unit managers have little cause to concern themselves on an ongoing basis with the level of deferred maintenance on the physical plant, with the annual investments made in equipment or library books, or with the ways in which the institution's funds are invested in the recruitment of a particular type of student body. This is especially true when these priorities conflict with investments in faculty and other personnel. It is the responsibility of executive-level administrators to ensure that the assets of the institution are protected and enhanced as necessary. When they fail to explicitly consider the size and characteristics of the institution's asset structure, the centerpiece of the strategic budget process, they voluntarily cede use of one of the most powerful tools of institutional change to those in no position to use it.

In the accounting sense, assets are defined as "probably future economic benefits obtained or controlled by a particular entity as a result of past transactions or events" (Wainright, 1992, p. 214). In the context of decisions encompassed by the strategic budgeting process, it is useful to consider the following as assets that must be created, maintained, and, over time, shaped to meet the emerging needs of the institution:

Faculty and staff. Human resources are not considered assets in accounting parlance. However, there are very few college administrators who will not admit, even passionately argue, that its people are a college's or university's most important resource. Further, when institutions of higher education hire regular employees of any type, these are investment decisions. Colleges and universities make social, if not legal, contracts with their regular employees and, in most cases, anticipate indefinite periods of appointment. In many institutions, the commitment often extends beyond the individual employee and attaches to the position filled by that individual.

There are groups of employees—those with temporary or adjunct appointments—to whom institutions do not make such long-term commitments. The budget decisions that surround expenditures for such personnel are more akin to decisions regarding purchase of personal services than to decisions regarding hiring of new employees. Decisions to hire employees on regular appointments are essentially investment decisions, whereas decisions to employ temporary staff or adjunct faculty are essentially decisions to conserve services at a particular level. This distinction between *investment* (in human assets) and *consumption* is maintained throughout this chapter.

Facilities. The physical plant owned by an institution is an asset in the classic accounting sense of the term. The decision to construct or to purchase facilities is an investment decision. Rental of facilities obligates an institution to a series of consumption expenditures.

Equipment. Like the physical plant, owned equipment is an institutional asset. The possibility of renting or leasing equipment rather than buying it again presents institutions with fundamental choices between investment and consumption.

Library collections. Library books, too, are institutional assets in at least the narrowest sense of the term. The rapidly escalating costs of books and periodical subscriptions, coupled with the advent of new technologies that allow access to information as an alternative to ownership of documents, will increase the necessity of looking seriously at the consumption versus investment decision.

Student body. Except in rhetorical terms, an institution's student body is seldom considered an asset. However, decisions concerning the clientele to be served are key strategic decisions for an institution, and considerable institutional energy is devoted to enrollment of a student body of a particular size and composition. Further, at many institutions, the investments made in acquiring a student body are exceeded in size only by the investments made in acquiring and retaining the faculty and staff of the institution. The great extent to which budgeting decisions in this area are left to the operational level and are disconnected from planning decisions regarding clientele made at the strategic level is a particularly curious phenomenon is a period of tightly constrained resources.

Endowments and reserves. Decisions regarding the size of surpluses to be built into the general fund budget, the extent to which resources are to be drawn down to balance the budget, and the size of the contingency reserve to be included as protection against unexpected events are truly strategic budgeting decisions. Decisions about these financial assets represent one of the few areas where institutional administrators have been engaged consistently at the strategic level.

Curricula. Curricula are another area in which institutions make sizable investments without recognizing the results as assets. Investments are not made directly in curricula; rather, they are made in faculty whose time is allocated to the creation of curricula. Failure to recognize curricula as assets has the unfortunate side effect of avoiding recognition that programs, like other assets, deteriorate over time. In the absence of continual attention to renewal, curricula can become institutional liabilities rather than assets.

Image and reputation. These two factors must be included on the list to draw attention to the fact that assets come in intangible, as well as tangible, forms. Further, these intangible assets are increasingly important to an institution. At a time when competition for students is increasing, any action or condition that sullies an institution's reputation or mars its image can be a serious problem. Investments in image and reputation run the gamut from public relations activities to much less visible efforts to ensure institutional actions consistent with role, mission, and educational philosophy.

The above-listed assets represent institutional capacity; the ways in which they are utilized determine educational outcomes and productivity. Institution-level managers must be held responsible for ensuring that capacity appropriate to the institution's mission is created and sustained. In the final analysis, unit managers are responsible for ensuring that these assets are utilized in ways that efficiently and effectively achieve the academic outcomes established as priorities for the institution.

In taking responsibility for the asset structure of an institution, institutional administrators must focus on requirements at two levels: the acquisition or creation of new assets and the maintenance of existing assets. In higher education, it is common practice to devote considerable time and energy to the creation of new assets and pitifully little to the maintenance of old assets. This is in spite of the fact that all assets depreciate and, without conscious attention, gradually lose their value to the institution. Buildings fall into disrepair, equipment and library books become outdated, and curricula are not revised to incorporate and integrate new knowledge. Personnel, too, can gradually lose their ability to be fully contributing members of the institutional community. Thus, wise administrators are concerned with staff development activities and the need for faculty to have time to recharge their intellectual batteries through sabbaticals, scholarly activities, or other mechanisms.

While the concept of asset depreciation is acknowledged by most campus-level administrators, the allocation of resources to counteract the consequences of the passage of time often are assigned low priority. Even in the best of budgetary times, funds for personnel and program development, replacement of equipment, and renovation of the physical plant are seldom allocated in adequate amounts. Neither funders nor institutional administrators receive acclaim for the unglamorous acts of maintaining the value of the old; recognition attaches to those who create the new.

The decisions associated with creating (or shaping) an institution's assets are more numerous than are typically recognized in any formal sense. In the process of strategic budgeting, the following issues must be addressed:

Quantity of the asset. This is one of the decision areas in which administrators are most practiced. They are comfortable with decisions that focus on full-time equivalent (FTE) faculty, square feet of building, numbers of students, and size of the endowment. They are less likely to be engaged in determining quantities of equipment or of library collections except as those quantities are reflected in their financial equivalents.

Type of asset. Within most of the major categories of assets (financial resources being the obvious exception), there are subcategories representing distinctions that cannot be ignored. It is meaningless to deal with FTEs of personnel without distinguishing faculty from clerical staff or to determine physical plant needs without recognizing differences between laboratories and administrative offices. The ways in which personnel assets are shaped are a particularly important reflection of institutional philosophy and represent key strategic decisions. For example, institutions have the choice of delivering learning assistance services through academic departments (utilizing faculty) or through student services units (utilizing nonfaculty professionals). The choice that is made can affect not only the budget but also the way in which the institution is perceived by students and the image that is created in the external environment.

Quality of the asset. Issues of quantity represent commonplace considerations in the budget process; issues of asset quality are dealt with more by default than by advertence. The default condition tends to be the "highest quality" (as in faculty or student) or "state of the art" (in regard to equipment). Alternatives suggesting that assets be of a quality that is "appropriate" or "the minimum required to effectively serve the purpose" are seldom established as standards in higher education. As distasteful as it may be to accept quality standards expressed in this way, the choice is viable, and perhaps even necessary, for many institutions.

Levels of utilization of the asset. Expectations regarding levels of utilization of some of the primary assets (personnel and physical facilities, for example) are determinations that are central to the strategic budgeting process. When institutional policy regarding faculty teaching loads is established, a major budgetary decision is also made; the policy has a direct bearing on the number of faculty required to meet student demand.

Price of the asset. For many institutional assets, considerations of price are not within the decision domain of the institution. Prices of books, for example, are established by the publisher rather than the purchaser. With regard to some assets, however, institutions can establish price, at least within certain limits. Faculty salaries are dictated by the market only to a certain extent; institutions can choose how competitive they want to be within the range established by market mechanisms.

Method of acquiring the asset. Finally, strategic budget decision making encompasses a set of decisions about whether capacity is to be owned or rented. Capacity can be acquired through investment in an asset. It can also be acquired through purchase of a service (as when services of adjunct faculty are acquired to replace the services of full-time faculty or when access to information services is acquired as a substitute for the purchase of library resources) or through leasing buildings and equipment. It should also be noted that assets can be acquired through the process of conversion from one type of asset to another. Conversions occur frequently; faculty members become administrators, and classrooms are converted to microcomputer laboratories, for example.

This delineation of a set of institutional assets and of the basic dimensions of this set establishes a decision-making framework for strategic budgeting that is roughly summarized in Figure 1.1. This figure indicates several features of budget decision making at the strategic level. First, it recognizes the basic equation of budgeting: Revenues must equal expenditures. On the revenue side of the equation, it should be noted that budget making involves making decisions as well as making estimates. Decisions such as those that lead to intended changes in the revenue profile or to stabilizing the amount of revenue to be received from a particular source constitute a necessary ingredient of budgeting at the strategic level. Likewise, decisions to utilize resources to offset revenue shortfalls—essentially, to use reserves as sources of revenue—are strategic decisions.

On the expenditure side of the equation, the decisions revolve around not only the mix of assets and consumption items and their characteristics (quantity, quality, price, and so on) but also the trade-offs among these various elements. The price of faculty (their salaries) can be increased if their utilization (work load) can be increased and the quantity thereby reduced. Similarly, the price of faculty may have to be suppressed if it is determined that the number

Figure 1.1. Decision-Making Framework for Strategic Budgeting

	Expenditures					*Revenues*
	Quantity	*Quality*	*Utilization*	*Price*	*Total Cost*	
Assets						Tuition and fees
Faculty and staff						Government appropriation
Faculty						
Administrators						
Support						Government grants and contracts
Facilities						
Equipment						
Collections						Private gifts, grants, and contracts
Student body						
Endowments and reserves						
Curricula						Endowment income
Image						
						Sales and services
Consumption						
Faculty and staff						Other
Faculty						
Administrators						Transfer in (from reserves and so on)
Support						
Facilities						
Equipment						
Collections						
Curricula						
Supplies						
Utilities						
Other services						

of adjuncts must be reduced so that more freshman courses can be taught by full-time faculty. A layer of complication is added by interactions across types of assets. For example, it may be possible to reduce the overall long-term investment in faculty by increasing the short-term investment in curricula. By investing in restructuring of the general education core curriculum of the college, it may be possible to alter faculty work loads or the number of faculty required to meet student demand. Similarly, a strategic decision to change the undergraduate curriculum so that lower-division students are confronted with fewer large classes has repercussions not only for the faculty asset but potentially for facilities and library collection assets as well.

Implications of Strategic Budgeting

Adoption of the basic concept of strategic budgeting has significant implications for both the decision makers and the analysts involved in the budget-building process. The implications are perhaps greatest for those administrators with institutionwide responsibilities. Their role in the budget process becomes proactive, their basic decisions come early in the budget process, and they will be faced with decisions that cannot help but be unpopular in some instances.

The scope of the early decisions can be seen by referring again to Figure 1.1 and recognizing that it outlines the basic contents of the guidelines to be distributed to, and utilized by, unit managers as they build their budgets. This process requires institutional managers to go well beyond their typical steps of reporting revenue estimates and establishing the levels of price increases that will be tolerated in the requests forwarded by the unit heads. Adherence to the concept of strategic budgeting requires institutional administrators, as the individuals responsible for preserving the institution's assets, to declare the level of funding to be set aside for this purpose. In essence, the process is initiated by determining the amounts that will "come off the top" for such purposes as the purchase of equipment and library books and for the renewal and renovation of the physical plant. These allocations, therefore, are less likely to be treated as the sum of whatever remains after unit priorities are established. In addition, the process proscribes the degree of freedom allowed unit managers in making unit-level decisions that have institutionwide implications. The most critical of institution-level decisions involve the leeway allowed unit managers in making decisions about faculty: to unilaterally establish work load policies and, a more commonly encountered practice, to freely determine the substitution of part-time for full-time faculty. It should be noted that these guidelines do not serve as determinants for individual units; however, they do serve to constrain (or, in some cases, expand) the pool of resources for which units compete.

If logically extended, adoption of the concept of strategic budgeting serves to open the gates for discussion of topics that often are avoided, either knowingly or unknowingly, and to reclaim for institutional administrators a role in decisions that are frequently assumed to lie exclusively in the domain of unit administrators. Perhaps the best example of the point is found, again, in the role of institutional administrators in shaping the faculty asset. It is not uncommon to find situations in which the responsibilities of institutional administrators are deemed to end when positions are allocated and prices established. Decisions about the quality or qualities of the individuals hired to fill those positions are frequently left to the unit heads. In the absence of clear understandings between institutional and unit administrators as to sought-after characteristics, this bifurcation of decision-making authority can very easily lead to conditions in which qualities of the faculty employed serve to impede rather than promote achievement of the institutional mission. The classic example is the hiring by teaching institutions of faculty who have research activities as their primary professional interests. There are many other such examples in which the nature of institutional assets is inconsistent with institutional mission and culture.

Implementation of strategic budgeting affects unit heads as well as institutional heads. For deans, directors, and department heads, however, the nature of the effects can be quite varied. On the one hand, when institutional administrators assume explicit responsibility for the maintenance of assets, it is likely that the pool of resources set aside for purchasing books and equipment will be larger than would otherwise be the case. Unit managers typically prefer to relegate such purchases to a lower priority rather than confront strictures in other areas. The down side is that presentation of a more complete set of budget guidelines removes some decision-making latitude from the domain of unit managers. As noted previously, strategic budgeting does not determine allocation of resources to individual units. That decision is ultimately made through processes that originate at the unit level and work their way up. However, strategic budgeting goes further than is typically the case in specifying the size of the various resource pools for which unit heads eventually compete. In many ways, it could make the job of the unit managers more difficult. In some instances, standard responses to budget balancing—forgoing equipment and purchases and substituting part-time faculty for full-time faculty—could be precluded. More emphasis would likely be placed on issues of faculty quality and work load and of curriculum changes, all topics that most deans and department chairs would just as soon avoid.

Finally, the type of approach to budgeting described in this chapter can have a significant impact on the kinds of analyses done in support of the budget process. Relatively less attention is devoted to compiling information on asset prices, and relatively more energy is devoted to analyses of asset quality and utilization. In addition, the range of assets explicitly considered during the budget process is expanded. As a consequence, analyses that support decisions on the investments required to create or maintain assets such as collections, the student body, and curricula are required on a regular, though not necessarily annual, basis.

Summary

In this chapter, I have suggested the necessity of developing an approach to budgeting that encompasses a set of strategic as well as operational decisions. I have argued that strategic decisions focus on the creation and maintenance of institutional capacity, whereas operational decisions focus on the utilization of that capacity in ways designed to accomplish specified purposes. As a consequence, strategic budgeting must emphasize institutional assets and the steps that can be taken to move toward an asset profile appropriate to the institution.

Such an approach to budgeting places greater responsibilities on institutional-level administrators and forces them to be proactive rather than reactive in the resource allocation process. These steps lead to an altered distribution of decision-making authority, requiring changes in behavior by all engaged in the resource allocation. Such steps are necessary if linkages between budgeting and strategic planning are to be forged.

References

Caruthers, J. K., and Orwig, M. *Budgeting in Higher Education.* AAHE-ERIC/Higher Education Research Report, no. 3. Washington, D.C.: American Association for Higher Education, 1979.

Jones, D. P. *Higher Education Budgeting at the State Level: Concepts and Principles.* Boulder, Colo.: National Center for Higher Education Management Systems, 1984.

Wainright, A. "Overview of Financial Accounting and Reporting." In D. M. Green (ed.), *College and University Business Administration.* (5th ed.) Washington, D.C.: National Association of College and University Business Officers, 1992.

DENNIS P. JONES is president of the National Center for Higher Education Management Systems, Boulder, Colorado.

General education, often a cash cow for arts and sciences departments, can be ineffective and mask high costs in the departments' major programs.

The Cost of General Education

Robert P. Lisensky

The need to curtail costs has again become a dominant theme in higher education. This need is a by-product of a number of factors, such as demographics, competition, and fiscal trends, as well as more subtle concerns, such as a resolve to control unbridled expansionism, an unwillingness to continue to increase tuition faster than inflation, and a desire to stimulate growth in some areas and decrease it in others. The challenge of cost containment in higher education is not new; its most recent resurgence was in the mid 1970s. Yet it is highly probable that the primary issue for higher education in this decade will be how to curtail costs while maintaining quality.

General Approaches to Cost Containment

There have been three basic approaches to cost containment in higher education. The first is across-the-board reductions. Institutions spread whatever funds are available over all of the activities of the enterprise and, in so doing, achieve short-term stability at the cost of avoiding key decisions. The result is that "the strong get weak and the weak get weaker." The second approach is line-item reductions. The focus is on what can be targeted: book budgets, equipment, travel, and so on. Line-item reductions are often accompanied by salary and hiring freezes, which, because of the seemingly random nature of those who leave, affect the quality of both personnel and programs.

In both of the preceding approaches, the future of the institution is jeopardized because the basic assets of the institution are jeopardized: facilities, equipment, library, faculty development, student diversity, and so on. Because too little attention is given to maintaining assets, the basic infrastructure erodes—at an exponential pace, in most cases. Once atrophied, the infrastructure is very difficult to restore.

NEW DIRECTIONS FOR HIGHER EDUCATION, no. 83, Fall 1993   © Jossey-Bass Publishers   17

The third approach to cost containment, the elimination of academic departments, programs, and even schools or administrative units, seems more drastic. But its effect is often not dramatic, because the programs eliminated had few students or graduates. Typically, little thought is given to whether these programs are critical to the institutional mission or whether they may be needed in the future. A good illustration of this approach was the elimination or reduction of foreign language programs prior to the call for global awareness.

Administrative functions that are "cut" seldom really go away, since they are simply reassigned to other administrative offices. The great increase in administration in the last decade is the by-product of three factors: administrators who assume tasks once performed by faculty (counseling, advising, developmental education, and so on); growth in administrative staffs in response to external constituency demands (federal and state governments, state commissions, and so on); and increases in revenue-producing activities (admission, development, financial aid, and so on). These causes of growth will not go away. The problem with administrative reductions or simplifications is that the services curtailed are often client-centered. This approach is hard to defend if we in higher education seek to enhance our role as a service industry.

The problem with most academic pruning or administrative simplification is that it is not an exercise in mission clarification but a response to a set of political issues. Resource management should function to ensure that plans are implemented. This end can be very difficult to achieve for institutions of higher education that lack a sense of direction and purpose, that are not able to establish clear priorities for their goals, and that thus have difficulty maintaining priorities in the resource allocation process. They have not been able to define an institutional image; they have allowed "mission drift." When this occurs, financial decisions focus on balancing the budget, not on reinforcing a shared vision. In that process, budget decisions become unit decisions, not institutionwide decisions. The total institution is regarded as a collection of individual parts that can be added to, or subtracted from, depending on the power that the units can wield. To make things more difficult, the dominant management style in higher education, a consensus-building model, is not conducive to mission clarification.

Problems with Curriculum Structure: General Education

To be truly successful in containing costs, colleges and universities must develop a renewed sense of purpose. If "growth by substitution," "innovation by substitution," or "quality by substitution" is what will help us deal with the challenges of the 1990s, we shall need more than ever to understand our mission. For effective cost containment, it is critical to attend to the gestalt of an institution as well as its parts. We have become proficient in gathering data and information about the effectiveness and efficiency of individual units. We have not been as successful in understanding the role of these individual units in defining and enhancing institutional purpose.

Curriculum structure is one of the areas that needs to be reviewed from both integrative and program perspectives. The Association of American Colleges (1985) maintained that the curriculum requires a structure that does more than respond to students' interests, or major and general distribution requirements. The problem is not a lack of curriculum structure but rather that the structure does not always make sense. This is especially true for general education. There have recently been numerous attempts to gather information about general education. These studies have taken various approaches, for example, reviews of the changes in general education requirements and attempts to determine the effects of general education. Probably one of the more ambitious projects is under way at the University of Pennsylvania, which is developing a liberal arts data base in order to provide sample measures of the curriculum's shape, organization, structure, and coherence (Zemsky, 1989).

Most of these studies of general education attempt to answer only the first of the three questions typically used in program review: "Does the program do any good?" The answer is almost always yes. Criticism of general education emphasizes inadequacies, not appropriateness. General education is an issue of widespread concern because the programs are not doing enough good. The major concern is that general education is not a program but a collection of courses separated from the mainstream of departmental offerings. The second question in program review is seldom asked: "Is the good worth the cost?" Little seems to be written about the cost of general education because it is automatically assumed that it is a cash cow—large classes, high student-faculty ratios, taught by poorly paid graduate students or often by faculty who need required courses to generate student loads. Seldom is there conversation about how the structure of the general education program affects the cost of upper-division courses in the arts and sciences or about the noneconomic cost of diverting the institution from its basic mission. Although little attention is directed to the second question, the third question is hardly ever asked: "Can you get the good for less cost?" If higher education really must learn to do more with less, this question must also be asked in relation to general education.

General education requirements are a major part of a student's program. The American Council on Education's (1990, p. 3) survey of campus trends showed that 77 percent of the public four-year institutions required 30 percent or more of the total credits in general education (23 percent required 40 percent or more), and 85 percent of the independent four-year institutions required 30 percent or more (46 percent required 40 percent or more). Studies indicate that in the last ten years the components of general education are increasing in number. There has been increased interest in freshman seminars and senior capstone courses, but the real increases have been in the basic skills (oral and written communication, mathematical competence, and, in some cases, listening). There is also a new interest in identifying an additional set of higher-order skills (critical thinking, problem solving, data gathering and synthesis, and creative thinking). If one adds to this domain concern for science and technology, ethnic and gender studies, and global awareness, it is easy to understand why more than one-third of a student's courses are in general education. As more campuses debate the nature of the goals of general education—basic skills, higher-order skills, interdisciplinary teaching, and new areas of general knowledge—the number of general education requirements will increase.

Over the years, as my colleagues and I at the National Center for Higher Education Management Systems (NCHEMS) have helped institutions deal with cost containment or curtailment, we have become more aware of the problems that are the result of curriculum structure. The data that we have gathered indicate the need for more sophisticated fiscal analysis of general education. For example, reviewing the expenditure patterns of a public four-year technical institution, which offered both associate and bachelor's degrees, we found that the structure of the curriculum was challenging the mission of the institution. The distribution requirements were structured in such a way that 65 percent of all lower-division student credit hours were generated by the School of Arts and Sciences (Figure 2.1). If the lower-division credit hours taught by the Schools of Technology, Business, and Allied Health for their associate degree programs had been treated as courses in the majors, the percentage of lower-division student credit hours taught by arts and sciences faculty would have been significantly higher. From the point of view of class size or total credit hours generated, there did not seem to be a problem. However, the School of Arts and Sciences, although generating significant student credit hours, conferred approximately 16 percent of the associate degrees and only 6 percent of the bachelor's degrees.

General education should take different forms in institutions with different missions. In the case of the above-cited technical institution, the freshman and sophomore curricula reflected a typical liberal arts college program. The lower-division curriculum had unintentionally been captured by or delegated to the School of Arts and Sciences. Over the years, the institution had increasingly moved further from its mission. Many decisions had been made that refuted its role as a technical university. To reverse this trend, a number of approaches might be taken without sacrificing the commitment to general education. Courses in technology might be substituted for the natural sciences requirement, or interdisciplinary courses in science and technology could be created. The curriculum could also be structured to enable students to take courses in their major during the first two years. New combinations of majors and minors could be created (for example, a business major and a technology minor), along with a fusing of practical and academic education. The success of the institution depends on its ability to maintain its competitive advantage, that of being a technical institution, which has already been

Figure 2.1. Sample Percentages of Student Credit Hours (SCH) in Undergraduate Programs, by Division

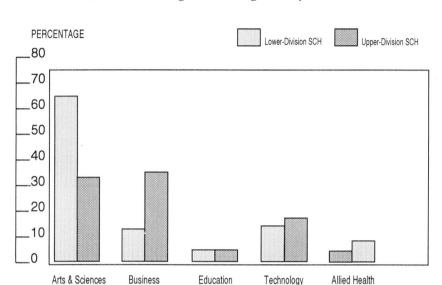

eroded. In this case, there are two cost questions: the economic cost and the cost of losing the institution's distinctiveness.

Problems with curriculum structure surface in similar ways in different types of institutions. This is true especially in institutions where the majors are predominantly in professional fields, a category that includes the vast majority of the institutions of higher education, public or private. In a public four-year urban university that NCHEMS assisted, 72.9 percent of the student credit hours generated were lower-division credits (Figure 2.2). Of the student credit hours generated by the College of Arts and Sciences, 83.9 percent were lower-division credits. The College of Arts and Sciences generated a significant number of credit hours, yet, in the last five years, less than 13 percent of the bachelor's degrees awarded have been from that college. As a result of that work load and a reduction in state funding, 24 percent of the student credit hours generated by arts and sciences were by part-time faculty. Moreover, it was in the basic skills area of the distribution requirements that the greatest number of student credit hours were generated by part-time faculty (English, 41.8 percent; foreign language, 33.9 percent; communications, 37 percent; sociology, 32.6 percent; mathematics, 31.8 percent). The cost for this institution is a full-time arts and sciences faculty that does not teach the lower-division courses and does not have enough students for the upper-division courses or graduate work offered. This curriculum structure is also one of the factors responsible for a high attrition rate in the first two years.

**Figure 2.2. Sample Percentages of Lower-Division and
Upper-Division Student Credit Hours Generated:
Total Institution Versus Arts and Sciences**

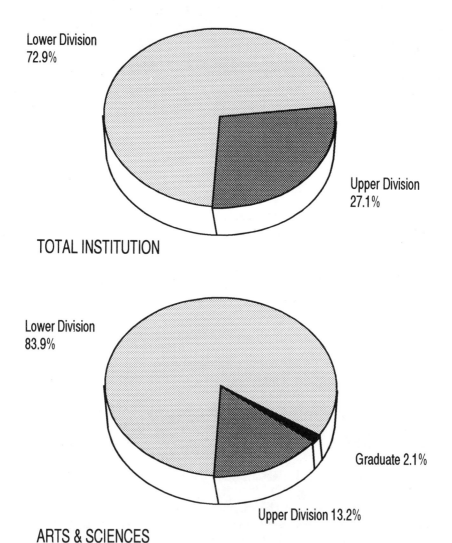

Lower Division
72.9%

Upper Division
27.1%

TOTAL INSTITUTION

Lower Division
83.9%

Graduate 2.1%

Upper Division 13.2%

ARTS & SCIENCES

The curriculum structure at a private four-year urban university created a similar problem. The university had a distinctive general education program that consumed a high percentage of a student's program in both the freshman and sophomore years. The majority of the students obtained professional degrees. Typically, about 68 percent of the bachelor's, 83 percent of the master's, and 70 percent of the doctoral degrees awarded were professional degrees (business, education, social work, law, and so on). The combination of a specially designed general education program offered primarily by the arts and sciences faculty and professional graduate programs with a smattering of master's and doctorate programs in the arts and sciences created an imbalance in the number of small classes offered by the institution at the upper-division level (Figure 2.3). Over 45 percent of all upper-division courses had less than ten students; 64.8 percent of the arts and humanities, 56 percent of the natural sciences, and 50 percent of the mathematics and computer science upper-division courses had less than ten students. This institution, when compared with a designated peer group, had the highest total revenue and the highest expenditure for instruction, while faculty salaries in all categories were significantly below the peer average.

The concern for curriculum structure also was an issue for a small private liberal arts college assisted by NCHEMS. As indicated in Figure 2.4, less than 10 percent of the teaching hours in speech, philosophy, history, and American studies were taken by majors in the respective departments. It is not hard to identify the required general education areas that might be pruned if the institution was required to do more for less.

Curriculum Reform, Institutional Effectiveness, and Cost Containment

In all but one of the four institutions cited above there were discussions about developing additional distribution requirements, which would increase the work load of the arts and sciences faculty. These examples are not offered as an indictment of general education, for it is a critical dimension of the learning process, nor as an indictment of arts and sciences. The objective is to encourage a conception of general education not as a collection of separate courses from the various disciplines or as a program, but as an integrated part of the total education experience.

The question still remains, How can we get the good for less cost? There are a number of possibilities. First, *the information base about the curriculum structure must be enhanced.* Data must be gathered about specific programs (major, distribution requirements) from an institutionwide perspective. It is not enough to gather information about student credit hours in the departments, or student credit hours in those courses required in general education; it is important as well to understand the relationship of each to the other and the impact that they have on each other. To determine better ways of getting

Figure 2.3. Sample Percentages of Small Classes in Traditional Undergraduate Programs, by Division

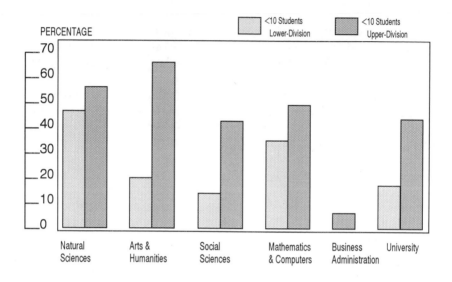

Figure 2.4. Sample Percentages of Student Credit Hours Taken by Majors and Nonmajors in a Liberal Arts Curriculum

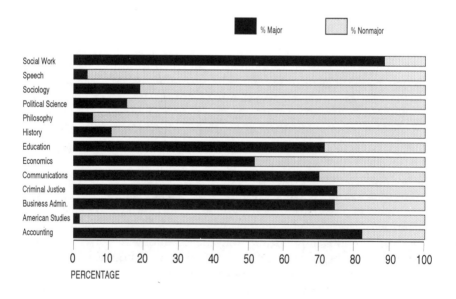

the good, we have to understand what is happening in the curriculum now. Knowledge about what the curriculum structure *is* enhances the collective understanding of what it is not and what it should be. Information must be gathered about general education as a program (which is seldom done) and also about the manner in which it is integrated with the institution's undergraduate curriculum as a whole. Information is the key to effectiveness whether we are discussing financial or academic effectiveness. An informed faculty is the strongest potential force for change in higher education.

Second, *the governance structure of general education must be changed.* Currently, there are two layers of academic management: the divisions and the institution. Either the responsibility for general education is given over to the divisions or it falls somewhere between the layers of management. A group of faculty drawn from the divisions is usually responsible for the quality of general education. Very seldom is the program the responsibility of any single individual, though there are signs that this governance structure is beginning to change. However, for this change to work, the program director must have the power to negotiate arrangements for compliance and have the resources to provide incentives for change. The program needs its own budget and a separate recognition and reward system.

Third, *rational inconsistencies must be encouraged.* Like all organizations, higher education overbureaucratizes implementation and undermines innovation. The more bureaucratic an organization becomes in its operation, the more comfortable are its participants because all responses are predictable. Academic departments and specialization have come to control institutions of higher education. Because of this, Irvin (1989) has revitalized an old idea: Create a separate faculty for general education, divorced from faculty in the departments. He recommends that general education be treated as a disciplinary subject. The problem with this approach is that it reinforces the division between the majors and general education. This approach assumes that there is no possibility of a fusion between practical and academic learning. What is lost is the possibility of enriching the majors and integrating general education. The culture of higher education necessitates that the departmental structure become a part of the reform of curriculum structure; it cannot be circumvented.

An alternative to complete separation is to understand that it is entirely rational for institutions to have different criteria for hiring in different areas, and that there might be different criteria for quality. The commitment to quality faculty usually is related not to the appropriateness of faculty skills to the functions performed but rather to a set of traditional criteria. The hiring of English department faculty who meet the qualifications for research and graduate education, or who have specialized in literature when a vast amount of work is in lower-division writing courses, provides the basis for problems not only of morale but also of curriculum structure.

All of the above three changes can affect the quality and cost of general education without curriculum change. The fourth suggestion focuses on a much more sweeping change, the *development of an integrated academic plan*. The typical response to the need to develop an additional set of basic or higher-order skills, and to the need to encourage attitudinal changes in students, is to introduce another course rather than to obtain a broad-based commitment from the community to respond to these needs throughout the curriculum, and to value them as skills or attitudes that are enhanced through use in all areas of the curriculum, including discipline-based courses. Not only basic skills but higher-order skills and values must be taught across the curriculum.

Conclusion

The normal discipline-based organizational structure of colleges and universities must be transcended. General education should be an integral dimension of professional education, not an isolated, separate learning experience. The structure of the curriculum should consist of more than a required number of courses for general education and the major; the curriculum should include courses intentionally interrelated in coverage and expectation.

It is important to understand both the financial and noneconomic costs of general education not so much to reduce expenditures as to free resources for enriching undergraduate education—having classes small enough to encourage active exchanges between students and faculty and encouraging group projects, hands-on courses, freshman and senior seminars, front-loaded support services for freshmen, and so on. The Pew Foundation (1991, p. 1) project report states that "there are signs of a new willingness to examine how instruction should be delivered, how learning should be assessed, how the curriculum should be organized, how institutions should evaluate and reward successful teaching." It is possible that an understanding of the various costs of current general education programs will provide additional information to support that reform.

References

American Council on Education. *Higher Education and National Affairs.* Washington, D.C.: American Council on Education, 1990.
Association of American Colleges. *Integrity in the College Curriculum: A Report to the Academic Community.* Washington, D.C.: Association of American Colleges, 1985.
Irvin, G. "Pros and Cons: A Separate Piece for General Education." *Change,* 1989, 21 (14), 6–9.
Pew Foundation. *Policy Perspectives,* 1991, 4 (1), 1–8.
Zemsky, R. *Structure and Coherence: Measuring the Undergraduate Curriculum.* Philadelphia: Institute for Research on Higher Education, University of Pennsylvania, 1989.

ROBERT P. LISENSKY *is president of the National Center for Higher Education Management Services, Boulder, Colorado, and former president of Willamette University.*

Overhead costs are often charged to programs indiscriminately while the support activities that underlie those costs remain unanalyzed.

Activity-Based Costing: A Cost Management Tool

Frederick J. Turk

Most enterprises today—in corporate America, in government, and in the nonprofit sector—have concluded that self-examination is necessary to determine how they should change if they are to compete effectively in a rapidly changing economy. Competition for resources, for customers, and for markets is the driving force that gives leadership today pause for self-reflection.

Institutions of higher education are not excluded from this period of turmoil. Federal and state funding has been cut, in some cases dramatically. Competition for federal research dollars and for contributions from private donors and foundations is fierce. In the public sector, tuition increases have been substantial to offset significant reductions in state funding. In the private sector, tuition is a major funding source supporting operations. Tuition increases in this sector have been mitigated somewhat by governing boards because of concerns that independent institutions are pricing themselves out of the market. Student aid in this sector, however, has increased rapidly as institutions find that they must provide greater amounts of aid to attract and retain quality students. In too many cases, these discounts on tuition are an essential enticement to fill classrooms.

In summary, financial status and budgets are under the microscope at most institutions—public and private, large and small, well endowed and tuition-dependent. In every case, administrators face serious questions regarding the future financing of their enterprise's mission. Clearly, more resources are necessary to satisfy the programmatic appetites of higher education institutions. In going through this process of self-examination, it is clear that institutions must look at their cost bases, understand their cost structures, and determine how their resources, that is, people, facilities, and

   27

finances, can be used more effectively and efficiently to achieve their missions, goals, and objectives. This chapter proposes that institutions need a new tool to assess their cost structures. This cost management tool is called *activity-based costing*.

Responding to Changing Economic Conditions

Colleges and universities faced with budget shortfalls for the reasons just noted must initiate changes in order to live within the bounds of their available funds. The responses that institutions make to the changing economic conditions can be classified into four basic stages. For the moment, I focus on the first three stages, which are the typical responses that we observe at many colleges and universities.

Stage 1 is the *freeze* period. Here, senior management concludes that to save money, it is necessary to stop filling vacant positions, to reduce or eliminate salary increases, and to curtail travel, training, and other discretionary costs.

Stage 2 is the *cuts* stage, which is more serious than stage 1, since schools and departments are asked to reduce their budgets by 5, 10, or 15 percent. In comparison to the freeze period, the budget reductions are more stringent at this stage and typically are applied across the board, with everybody sharing the pain of retrenchment. By and large, these cuts begin to damage the academic or support capacity of the institution and erode its ability to provide the robust services that were available in the past.

Stage 3 entails the *downsizing* of the institution. As the term implies, this stage involves selected reductions in certain areas of the institution. In downsizing, greater emphasis usually is placed on the administrative functions. The focus on administration is based on the assumption that the academic programs are the lifeblood of the institution and therefore should be the last to be reduced. When it is concluded that certain academic programs and departments must have faculty reductions, early retirement programs may be initiated to induce faculty departures. Often, however, to the detriment of the institution, faculty whom the institution might wish to retain also take advantage of the retirement program opportunity.

Across these three stages, the responses to the changing economic situation produce important short-term savings that appear to keep the budget in balance, with the hope that things will quickly turn around. The reality is, however, that such reductions often are short-sighted and lack thoughtful consideration of the long-term future. The result in the long run is a cycle of decay because students and faculty eventually conclude that their institution is lacking in resources and is weakened. What is lacking is a clear vision of what the future institution should look like, an understanding of its basic cost structure, and a willingness to make important cost management decisions.

Sea Change in Enterprise Behavior

What we are seeing today in some institutions that wish to master their own futures is a discernible sea change in enterprise behavior. Generally, constituents of organizations today expect, and in many cases demand, that the enterprises do business differently. Although no one is happy about the need for change, most recognize that some shift in mind-set is essential if their institution is to compete successfully in the marketplace, whether the field of operation is corporate America, selling products, or higher education, providing essential instruction and research services. In essence, the time is right for institutions of higher education to bring all constituencies together to make meaningful changes that will benefit higher education in the years ahead.

The result of this change in behavior is a growing awareness on the part of leadership that future success for an institution depends on the achievement of *enterprise excellence*. Enterprise excellence is stage 4, a more sophisticated and thoughtful process of responding to the changing economic environment referred to earlier.

Achieving excellence in higher education requires a critical evaluation of academic and support activities in order to understand the current state of the institution. This analysis must be followed by a resolve to make meaningful change. The key question is, Change for what purpose? Change for change's sake will not achieve excellence. Rather, the institution must have a "reshaping vision," that is, a clear idea of what the college or university stands for and how it plans to provide select services. A reshaping vision describes the future mission, goals, and objectives of the institution and guides leadership and all constituencies in the allocation of resources to achieve excellence.

Implicit in the transformation of the institution from its current state to the shape envisioned is the need to restructure the enterprise and to reengineer the activities performed. These two transformational objectives typically require the introduction of continuous quality improvement as part of the new institutional culture and, simultaneously, reduction of costs and reallocation of savings to support high-priority needs. This form of resource transfer is euphemistically called *growth by substitution*.

Cost reductions are achieved by changing the activities of organizational units so that work is performed more efficiently and effectively. Productivity improvements and thus cost reductions can be achieved by such activity redesign. For many institutions, more significant improvements in productivity and quality of service are possible when technology is applied to speed processing, eliminate redundant and unnecessary work, and provide information rapidly to better serve students, faculty, and others and to provide timely information to support decision making.

Activity-Based Costing as a Cost Management Tool

How does activity-based costing (ABC) fit into the restructuring and reengineering needed to achieve a reshaping vision? As was just described, the process of transformation requires an understanding of the institution's work activities—both the current and the proposed restructured and reengineered activities. What is necessary is a system or process for evaluating the cost of current activities that can serve as the basis for making proposed changes. This process—ABC—must be based on a thorough review of the component activities involved in providing services so that their importance can be judged. An understanding of activity costs facilitates evaluation of proposed alternative resource decisions by explaining the cost implications of each alternative under consideration.

The ABC system establishes a basis for building an activity budget for the proposed restructured and reengineered enterprise. Cost measures for each activity can be developed to monitor activities over time to determine whether there are substantive variances from the activity budget.

Costing Problems

One significant problem faced by most institutions is that they do not know much about their costs. Caught in this cost trap, leaders, the governing board, and other constituencies have difficulty understanding why costs continue to rise so rapidly and what can be done to change cost behavior.

The basic budget control system in every institution is the financial accounting system. Its primary purpose is to help the institution fulfill its fiduciary responsibility of keeping track of funds received from third parties (the fund accounting system). The system also serves as a financial control system, organized by budget units that typically follow the organization of vice presidential areas, with academic and administrative departments and restricted grants and contracts separately identified. Institutions are captives of their financial accounting systems. The financial accounting system is influenced greatly by the fund accounting system and budget organization structure. The financial accounting system does not provide information that supports decisions regarding the effective and efficient allocation of resources. Thus, it does not highlight productivity variances or provide the grist for thoughtful analysis and decisions regarding changes that should be made.

Some institutions have established costing systems to help them better understand their costs. In fact, in the late 1970s, costing and cost information was deemed essential to the effective and efficient management of colleges and universities. Many institutions adopted the costing model established by the National Center for Higher Education Management Systems. Since then, these costing systems appear to have fallen into disrepair or to have been abandoned in many institutions.

Further, in the resource allocation cultures of many institutions, the current budget is accepted as the base for starting the next budget cycle. Primary attention is given to discussing and negotiating increments of the budget base with little attention given to the base. Only recently, as institutions have begun to go through the stages referred to earlier, are we seeing reductions in their budget bases. As was stated earlier, these reductions are often unsophisticated attempts to reduce costs, with little attention given to enterprise excellence.

Traditional Costing Systems

Traditional costing systems have tended to focus on capturing costs initially in the financial accounting system according to organizational budget units. In higher education, academic departments and sponsored grants and contracts represent budget units and are the entities that deliver the mission-related services of the institution, that is, instruction, research, and public service. Overhead departments such as plant operations and maintenance, finance, admissions, and registrar provide essential support to academic departments, helping them to carry out their responsibilities.

The traditional costing system abstracts cost information from the financial accounting system and allocates overhead support costs to the benefiting department and grants and contracts accounts. Examples of the allocation factors often used are salaries and wages to attribute finance department cost, square feet of assigned space to attribute plant operations and maintenance cost, and credit hours produced by instructors to attribute registrarial cost to academic departments and grants and contracts as appropriate.

What's wrong with the traditional costing model? It assumes that academic departments and grants and contracts caused the cost to occur. While, ultimately, it is true that they benefited from the support service received, there are other factors that influenced the magnitude of the cost being attributed. Because allocations are made, the cost information focuses primary attention on the direct costs of people, facilities, travel, and so on that are accumulated in academic departments and sponsored grants and contracts. On the flip side, because we merely allocate using imputed factors assumed to be related to the supporting activities, there is insufficient attention given to where the costs actually come from—the overhead support departments.

Activity-Based Management: The Why and How

An activity-based management system has at its center an ABC system. ABC was inspired by the work of faculty at the Harvard University Business School. Their work focused on the costing of products produced by manufacturing companies. Essentially, they observed that the traditional costing methodologies applied by these companies provided misleading messages about the cost of products. That resulted in inappropriate pricing decisions and value judgments regarding the profit contributions of different products.

Traditional costing systems assume that individual products cause costs, and, therefore, the system attributes resources consumed directly to products. The ABC system, on the other hand, traces costs, first, to the supporting activities as initial consumers of resources; these costs are subsequently attributed to products based on the relationship of the activities to the products produced.

To illustrate the application of the ABC system, one can study the admissions department in a university. Typically, the cost of admissions is accumulated in a single department in the form of budget lines for personnel costs of salaries and benefits and other budget lines for items such as supplies, travel, postage, and printing of materials. The ABC system asks the following questions: How are people spending their time and what other costs are incurred in performing the admissions function?

The ABC system requires, first, a definition of the major activities being carried out by the department, for example, recruiting and inquiry response, application processing, acceptance and follow-up, and communications. The costs traceable to the first-stage activities are determined by the analysis of personnel effort to determine if people spent 100 percent of their time performing one of these activities or if they split their time, say, 50-25-25 among three activities. In this case, the cost may be traceable to one activity or it may be split among the three activities. Similarly, other costs of supplies, travel, and the like are traced to one or more of the activities based on use.

To complicate the example somewhat, each of the activities noted supports the achievement of certain business processes: student marketing (creating the customer) and student matriculation (completing the sale) functions. First-stage drivers of cost describe the beneficial relationship between the activities and the business processes performed. In the example, the following relationships may be found: (1) The total effort, or 100 percent, of the recruiting and inquiry response activity benefits the student marketing business process. (2) The application processing activity benefits both student marketing and student matriculation and should share the costs based on the proportional relationship of applications processed in the marketing cycle and in the matriculation cycle. (3) The acceptance and follow-up activity benefits student matriculation 100 percent. (4) The communications activity benefits both student marketing and student matriculation and should share the costs based on the proportional relationship of pieces mailed for recruiting and inquiry response, application processing, and acceptance and follow-up.

Once the cost of the business processes is determined, it is necessary to attribute cost to schools, departments, or both. A second-stage driver of cost that describes what caused the cost to occur based on school or departmental consumption of the output of the business processes is determined. For student marketing, the number of students applying to a school or field of study drives the tracing of costs to the benefiting schools or departments. Student matriculation costs are traced to the benefiting schools or departments based on the number of freshmen and transfer students enrolled by the school or field of study.

Measures of the student marketing cost per student applying and the student matriculation cost per student enrolled are determinable through this calculation. This is information that is often not easily available but should be useful in determining the strategy and tactics associated with these very important business processes. In a similar fashion, the cost per applicant and matriculant for the activities identified in the first stage can be determined, analyzed, and used to consider changes in the application of personnel time and funds to carry out the activities.

Institutional Reengineering

ABC supports the process of reengineering the institution. It is essential to understand the costs and outputs of the activities performed in support departments. With this cost information, alternative approaches to performance of the activities can be identified. As these alternative approaches are defined, the cost of each can be determined using the ABC process. Opportunities for cost reduction are identifiable along with the changes in output from the newly constituted or modified activity construct being considered.

While the principal purpose of the ABC methodology is to more accurately assign overhead costs to final cost objectives (that is, products or, in higher education, schools and academic departments), the same system can be used to analyze the cost behavior of activities. Activity reengineering is achieved by deciding to apply resources differently through one or more of the following actions: change the flow and process of work, modify the work schedule, increase training to improve productivity or quality, simplify the work performed, combine fragmented activities, automate and eliminate manual work, standardize the work performed to eliminate or reduce exception processing, eliminate duplication or redundancy of work, and eliminate causes of error and rework.

Examples of reengineering activities include eliminating multiple approvals of transactions, avoiding errors in suspense accounts that require extensive analysis and correction, and combining activities to smooth the flow of work.

How to Make It Work

In order to make activity-based management an integral part of the way in which the institution manages its resources, four factors must be in place:

Urgency to act. Senior management and the governing board should perceive a need to change the way in which the institution carries on its affairs. Without such an expressed need, the motivation to collect and understand information on the cost of activities does not exist.

Reshaping vision. As part of the process of self-evaluation, leadership should develop a sense of how they would like the institution to look and behave in the future. This vision will define the actions that should be taken to change the way work is performed.

ABC analysis. A system needs to be established along the lines of the construct presented earlier to define activities, determine their cost, and assess their outputs. This ABC information then should be used to examine the implications of the reengineering changes that are being considered.

Just do it. Management must make the hard decisions and get it done. Once the analysis is completed, inaction can be detrimental to the long-term future of the institution. Change is difficult for all involved. It is essential to communicate the action that will be taken and to proceed swiftly.

Conclusion

The time has come for institutions to examine themselves to determine if they are using their resources most effectively. Competition is affecting higher education, just as it affects other organizations in our society. Ineffective use of resources drives up costs, which in turn cause tuition and fees to rise and require ill-advised cuts in academic programs and support activities. The long-term result is institutional decay and loss of reputation in the competitive marketplace.

Activity-based management of scarce resources helps ensure that all activities are operating at peak effectiveness and efficiency to achieve enterprise excellence. Both this approach to management and ABC should be integral parts of the accounting system for colleges and universities as they face the twenty-first century.

FREDERICK J. TURK is a partner at KPMG Peat Marwick in New York City.

Restructuring can entail alternative approaches to revenue generation as well as reallocation of internal resources.

Strategic Restructuring: A Case Study

James A. Hyatt

Every several years, in response to one crisis or another, a new planning or budgeting process comes along, appearing to be the panacea for higher education's woes. In the 1970s, it was long-range planning and zero-base budgeting. In the 1980s, the promising techniques were strategic planning and environmental scanning. Budget rescissions in the 1980s also produced a myriad of reallocations and retrenchment studies. These techniques stressed a reassessment of institutional role and mission and caused some institutions to reassess and reorder their priorities. Successful application of these approaches required institutional leadership and a commitment to "stay the course." Unfortunately, a number of institutions embraced, then rejected, these techniques, announcing that they were not really applicable to the complex environment of higher education.

In the last few years, faced with budget reductions and shrinking resource bases, again a number of institutions are examining ways of downsizing their operations. Independent institutions suffering from declining enrollments and under scrutiny for tuition increases that exceed inflation are going on a "revenue diet." Public institutions have seen their budgets reduced and are planning for "strategic contraction." Other institutions are repositioning themselves to respond not only to diminishing resources but also to new challenges and opportunities.

A major concern frequently expressed about higher education's fascination with alternative planning techniques is that colleges and universities tend to react to the symptoms of a disease rather than attempt to cure the disease. Higher education is not unique in this regard. According to a report on quality and cost containment from the University of Michigan, "The equivalent transformation in industry thinking about quality has been to move from viewing it as an inspection problem, to an assurance problem, to a management problem, to a strategic opportunity. This series of changes has occurred over approximately sixty years. In the University, it is imperative we follow a less circuitous path, and travel it more rapidly" (Task Force on Costs in Higher Education, 1990, p. 18).

Recognizing that structural rather than cosmetic changes were necessary if the campus is to position itself for the future, the University of Maryland at College Park has initiated a process of *strategic restructuring*. Strategic restructuring involves an assessment of existing approaches to revenue generation and resource utilization. Based on this assessment, alternative approaches to resource generation as well as ways to reallocate or redeploy existing resources are developed. To effectively implement a strategic restructuring process, an institution must not only conduct a thorough self-assessment but also have a set of clearly articulated priorities.

Strategic Restructuring at the University of Maryland at College Park

In preparing for the 1990s, the College Park campus developed an enhancement plan, which set institutional priorities in four major areas. Within each area, specific initiatives were identified along with an estimate of the resources necessary to achieve each initiative. First, the campus sought to continue its efforts to improve undergraduate education and enhance the quality of student life. As the state's flagship and major research institution, the campus also sought to strengthen its graduate and professional education programs. The second major area of enhancement involved strengthening of the institution's instructional and research programs. This initiative not only involved enhancement of select programmatic areas, such as interdisciplinary high-technology research programs and public policy and international affairs initiatives, but also sought to strengthen the campus core academic programs in the disciplines of the liberal arts and sciences. Moreover, the campus planned to upgrade the level of academic and institutional support, for example, in libraries and computing. The third and fourth major areas of enhancement included strengthening of campus outreach and public service programs and its administrative and institutional support programs. These four areas and their targeted initiatives defined the major campus priorities and agenda for the 1990s and beyond.

Given an ambitious enhancement plan, strategic restructuring became the catalyst for realigning campus resources to correspond with campus priorities. This realignment was achieved by examining four key components of institutional operations. These areas are outlined in Table 4.1.

Resources and Resource Generation. To begin the restructuring process, an institution must evaluate the ability of existing revenue sources to meet current and future demands. Financial projections or forecasts are extremely

Table 4.1. Strategic Restructuring at the University
of Maryland at College Park

Resources and Resource Generation	Resource Utilization	Management Processes and Procedures	Decision Making and Communication
Traditional resources	Patterns of resource utilization	Restructuring of existing management activities	Proactive versus reactive
Areas of opportunity	Financial flexibility	Procedural and organizational reform	Future-oriented versus retrospective
Full cost recovery	Analysis of source-use relationships	Customer versus bureaucratic orientation	Explicit versus implicit
Nontraditional resources		Training	Relationship of master plans to budgets

useful in developing this assessment. For example, a major factor that influenced Dartmouth College's decision to reduce costs was a financial forecast indicating that the campus could expect an $8 million deficit in three years. According to Dartmouth's president, James O. Freedman, "Every year, when the budget was out of balance, we always thought it was a one-year phenomenon" (McCurdy and McMillen, 1990, p. A35). Instead, the problem turned out to be symptomatic of escalating costs driven by both internal and external factors.

At the University of Maryland, a similar three-year financial forecast was prepared in the fall of 1990. This forecast proposed three funding scenarios: a worst case, a probable case, and a best case. The best-case scenario assumed that the present financial conditions were temporary and that the campus could anticipate a renewed commitment by the state to enhance funding of higher education. The worst- and probable-case scenarios assumed minimal or small increases in state support and projected that these increases would be used to offset inflation and maintain the base budget. More important, the worst- and probable-case scenarios indicated that any significant enhancement funding could not be derived from traditional sources of support, such as state appropriations or tuition and fee revenue; rather, it would have to come from internal reallocation or increased revenue from nontraditional sources.

In examining potential areas of opportunity for resource generation, the campus identified three areas in which additional revenue could be generated. First, the campus proposed to maintain and increase its fundraising and development activities. This strategy was viewed as an investment in the future. Second, the campus sought to recover fully all costs associated with services that it provided to other campuses within the University of Maryland system.

For example, the College Park campus had provided both facilities and services such as accounting and personnel services for its sister campuses. These services would now carry a price tag. Third, the campus began to explore how it could leverage its assets such as real estate holdings to either generate needed revenue or provide services to its students. In this regard, privatization of certain operations such as the operation of portions of its physical plant as well as partnerships with private developers was considered.

Outsourcing or privatization of institutional services and activities has also been considered by other institutions, including the campuses of the University of California. A report of the University of California (1991, p. 26) cites a model developed by Berkeley economist Oliver Williamson: "[The model] identifies a framework for making the outsourcing decision based on transaction costs. In this model, frequently occurring and nonspecific activities, such as fleet services, reprographics, and others may be logical candidates for outsourcing. Activities that are unique to the University, such as employee relations, should be operated in-house. Infrequently performed tasks of a somewhat specific nature might be performed by a vendor operating under a sole source agreement. Executive recruiting might be such an activity." While the analysis of alternative ways of generating revenues or providing services is still under development at the College Park campus, the strategic restructuring process has refocused the campus approach to revenue generation.

Resource Utilization. Together with the examination of approaches to resource generation, strategic restructuring also includes an assessment of how resources are utilized. Fundamental to this assessment is a thorough understanding of how resources have been utilized in the past. An important consideration is how the personnel compensation component of the budget drives the entire budget. For example, at most institutions of higher education, 80 to 90 percent of the budget is determined by expenditures for salaries and wages and benefits. The remaining 10 to 20 percent contains costs for base operations such as fuel and utilities that also are in large measure fixed and mandatory. As a consequence, the amount of budgetary flexibility at colleges and universities is quite small. Moreover, the degree to which faculty are tenured can limit the ability of a campus to restructure its academic programs. The ability of an institution to reduce expenditures in the short run is therefore limited, since such actions involve reduction or elimination of essential services and a drastic reduction in the number of staff.

Certain actions can alter resource utilization patterns. For example, early retirement programs, such as the Voluntary Early Retirement Incentive Program of the University of California, while having certain short-term and long-term costs, can create increased flexibility in the salary and wage component of campus budgets. Institutions can, and frequently do, choose to replace retiring personnel with more junior-rank faculty and staff. Furthermore, the mix of tenure- versus non–tenure track positions in various programs can be revisited in order to create budgetary flexibility. The departure of faculty from certain weaker or peripheral departments may also facilitate plans to merge or close departments. While these actions require the existence of a planning and priority-setting process on a campus, they are opportunities that can be capitalized on in an effective strategic restructuring process.

Another important element of the resource utilization component of strategic restructuring is an examination of the relationship between services provided and how services are funded. The base programs of an institution, such as instruction, public service, and academic and institutional support activities, are normally funded from education and general (E&G) revenues: tuition, mandatory fees, state appropriations, and other central unrestricted revenues. Other programs, such as auxiliary enterprises and dining and housing services, are usually established with the understanding that they should be self-supporting, that is, able to generate sufficient revenue from fees or sales of services to cover the operating costs. On some campuses, however, certain activities such as student health centers or public service activities both generate revenues from sales and services provided by the unit and receive an allocation of central E&G revenues.

Under strategic restructuring, all units are examined to determine whether the sources of revenue are appropriate to the programs or services provided. This examination frequently results in a restructuring of fund sources, which can result in changes in user fees to fully cover the services provided or an elimination or reduction of services provided. Any central funds that are released by such restructuring can then be applied to other institutional priorities. The resource utilization component of strategic restructuring is based on the principle that if resource utilization patterns are not reviewed on a routine basis, an institution can become locked into a fixed pattern of resource generation and use and therefore be ill prepared to meet future challenges and opportunities.

Management Processes and Procedures. Over time, an institution may be able to generate additional resources and improve its financial flexibility. If it fails, however, to examine and modify the manner in which services are provided, it will have achieved relatively little. Based on a recognition of this fact, strategic restructuring is designed to align the programs and services provided with the needs of the institution's customers. Strategic restructuring incorporates the process known as Total Quality Management (TQM) (see Coate, 1990). In fact, TQM is an integral component of the University of Maryland's strategic restructuring process.

Related to these actions is a thorough assessment of existing organizational processes and procedures. Frequently, a procedure will be required by a specific state or federal regulation. Over time, however, circumstances can change, and actions that were once necessary may no longer be required. Without an ongoing assessment of organizational processes and procedures, an institution may be using valuable resources to staff actions that are neither beneficial nor necessary. Internally, operating procedures can also yield results that run counter to their original intent. For example, as the University of California (1991, pp. 9–10) has stated, "At the operating level, past control strategies have created a plethora of rules, policies and procedures which are the source of many problems now experienced at the University. Ironically, these controls have not created any real control at all, only the illusion of control. In fact, this array of procedures focused at low levels in the organization promotes the misconception that as long as local units follow these 'procedures,' cost containment will just naturally happen and any cost overruns are central administration's problem." It is for this reason that procedures and policies should be reviewed from a unit or user perspective. In addition, according to Hyatt and Santiago (1986, p. 29), "Decisions should be made where most appropriate, that is, at the level having the necessary management and technical expertise and where the impact of the particular decision is greatest."

Strategic restructuring views management processes from a comprehensive campuswide perspective. This approach is necessary to move the campus forward as a whole rather than promote individual programs and activities. For example, a unit may try to be responsive to customer needs by enhancing or altering the manner in which services are provided. The impact of these actions, however, can be enhanced if other units with similar responsibilities are consulted and involved. Examples of initiatives that can benefit from a team approach to problem solving include student information and on-line registration systems, enrollment management, student retention, and recruitment activities.

Effective and enlightened management processes and procedures require an informed and involved staff. Ongoing training programs are essential to maintaining such a work force. In addition, unit participation in the development of training programs is essential. For example, over time, routine administrative processes and procedures can become institutionalized. As a consequence, they are frequently never questioned, and the institution continues to engage in business as usual. Only when a major problem occurs are such processes and procedures questioned, and by that time it is frequently too late to prevent major damage or disruption of services. To overcome this situation, routine training programs for all campus personnel should include a review of the rationale and justification for existing processes and procedures and should allow an opportunity for participants to offer suggestions for modifications or alternatives.

A dynamic management process can influence the manner in which resources are generated and utilized. Such a process promotes faculty and staff involvement and initiative. It also creates a culture that rewards individuals that are responsive and not resistant to change.

Decision Making and Communication. The fourth and perhaps key component of strategic restructuring is the development of decision-making processes that are more proactive than reactive. Too frequently, campuses react to a set of circumstances rather than take a proactive role in bringing about change. For example, when confronted with declining enrollments, a campus can either react to the demand by creating new or more marketable programs in an opportunistic manner or take a proactive stance and restructure or create programs to build on the institution's unique strengths and assets.

In a similar manner, decision making under strategic restructuring is directed toward future opportunities and challenges rather than recreation of the past. Instead of using an incremental approach to planning and budgeting, strategic restructuring considers both the base and the increment. Consequently, it tries to maximize the impact of strategic planning by applying a total resource concept to decision making. A total resource approach not only considers the impact of plans in terms of people, dollars, and space but also builds on an institution's strengths, for example, donor and alumni goodwill, distinction in instruction and research, and public service. It also capitalizes on such environmental factors as geography and relationships with industry and other institutions.

Regardless of the planning or budgeting technique used, the success of any process is based on effective communication. For example, are the outcomes of the planning and budgeting process communicated and clearly understood by campus decision makers and constituent groups? Too frequently, decision makers assume that their actions are explicit and can be readily understood by all concerned. In the absence of effective communication, however, the rationale underlying decisions is too frequently left to individual interpretation. To counteract this situation, a plan to communicate with all campus constituents, both internal and external to the institution, is a major component of strategic restructuring.

Strategic restructuring tries to link the discrete planning activities of an institution to an integrated planning and budgeting process. For example, the long-range facilities master planning process must recognize and accommodate the institution's academic plan, as do campus plans for fundraising and development, telecommunications, and information technology. Furthermore, an operating and capital budgeting process should build on divisional and departmental processes. A directive to create a central plan without the development of mechanisms for faculty, student, and staff involvement is a blueprint for failure. Although, conceptually, this advice appears sound, in reality budgeting and planning frequently occur in an ad hoc manner. For this reason, strategic restructuring emphasizes the need for interactive and ongoing communication among campus decision makers, from the chief executive officer to individual faculty, students, and staff.

Conclusion

Since the strategic restructuring process at the University of Maryland at College Park is only in its initial phase, the effectiveness of the process is yet to be determined. It is still not clear whether the restructuring will enable the campus to effectively respond to the current fiscal crisis or whether it will establish the mechanism needed to position the campus to respond to future challenges and opportunities. It is clear, however, that the incremental approach to planning and budgeting is not effective in planning for the future when resources are scarce and the costs of basic instruction and research are high. Strategic restructuring responds to the situation by taking a comprehensive approach that combines planning and budgeting with a more responsive and strategic approach to institutional management.

References

Coate, L. E. "TQM on Campus." *NACUBO Business Officer*, Nov. 1990, pp. 26–35.

Hyatt, J. A., and Santiago, A. *Financial Management of Colleges and Universities*. Washington, D.C.: National Association of College and University Business Officers, 1986.

McCurdy, J., and McMillen, L. "Stanford, Dartmouth Plan to Trim Size of Administration." *Chronicle of Higher Education*, Feb. 21, 1990, pp. A32, A35.

Task Force on Costs in Higher Education. *Enhancing Quality in an Era of Resource Constraints*. Ann Arbor: University of Michigan, 1990.

University of California. *Transforming the Administration at UCLA: A Vision and Strategy for Sustaining Excellence in the Twenty-First Century*. Los Angeles: University of California, 1991.

JAMES A. HYATT is associate chancellor at the University of California, Berkeley.

A Total Quality Management program, simple in concept, can improve staff morale as well as services to the institution's clients.

An Analysis of Oregon State University's Total Quality Management Pilot Program

L. Edwin Coate

Early in 1990, Oregon State University (OSU) set out to find its own answer to a question asked by a growing number of colleges and universities across the United States: How adaptable are the quality management methods of W. Edwards Deming, J. M. Juran, and Philip Crosby to higher education? It is obvious that manufacturing processes are far more predictable and controllable than the learning process. As OSU's top management explored Total Quality Management (TQM), they realized that TQM principles should not be applied without a period of research, adaptation, training, and testing in the actual university setting.

It was decided that testing could best be conducted in OSU's service functions, many of which have counterparts in industry; administrative units such as physical plant, business affairs, and printing and mailing could more readily adapt techniques of quality improvement to their processes. What was learned from their experience could then be applied to the more complex issues of adapting TQM to the university's academic side. The purpose of this chapter is to document OSU's TQM pilot program: its implementation, the teams' results, the evaluation survey, and the results of a cross-functional team formed to study and improve the pilot program.

TQM Pilot Program

Ten pilot teams were created to gain experience with TQM in OSU's environment before its techniques were applied more broadly.

New Directions for Higher Education, no. 83, Fall 1993 © Jossey-Bass Publishers

Hoshin **Planning.** During *hoshin*, or "breakthrough" planning, an initial step in implementing TQM, OSU's top management identified twelve critical processes basic to carrying out the university's mission. The vice president and the division directors for finance and administration followed the same process to identify critical processes for their unit and for each division. These processes constituted the basis for the work of the pilot TQM study teams (see Figure 5.1).

Pilot TQM Teams. OSU's early exploration of TQM had convinced management that teams are the very heart of TQM. Better solutions emerge, are implemented faster, and last longer when the people affected have helped to develop them.

Study teams are composed of people who normally work together on the process being reviewed. They are each led by someone from the natural work group, typically the supervisor, and are each assisted by a facilitator.

Teams usually work with processes that can be improved with resources they control. Teams are kept small (no more than ten members), and each has a sponsor, usually the group's division director. The sponsor ensures that the team's work is linked to the university's critical processes and moves the university toward its vision.

Ten Teams Formed. The divisions of finance and administration formed ten pilot TQM teams (Table 5.1). Each sponsor assigned the team a study issue or problem related to one of the division's critical processes.

Leaders and facilitators of the teams received about eighteen hours of training in TQM from a consultant. The consultant and the university's staff development officer then served as coaches, providing just-in-time training to team members as they moved through TQM problem-solving steps.

Ten-Step Problem-Solving Process. OSU teams used a ten-step TQM problem-solving model to guide their study (Figure 5.2). The process begins with the customer, focuses on root causes of problems, and ensures that decisions and actions are based on real data.

1. At the sponsor level, opportunities for improvement that relate to the team's critical process are identified and team members who have ownership in that process are selected.
2. Key customers are surveyed to find out which services provided by the process are not meeting their expectations.
3. The most important customer issue or problem is selected, and a clear issue statement is prepared.
4. A flow diagram is prepared, showing the process as it is.
5. A process performance measure is established to track progress in meeting or exceeding customer expectations.
6. Probable causes of the problem are identified, using tools such as the "fish-bone" diagram.
7. Real-time data on the probable causes are gathered to establish a benchmark against which to measure future progress.

Figure 5.1. OSU Critical Processes: Finance and Administration Detail

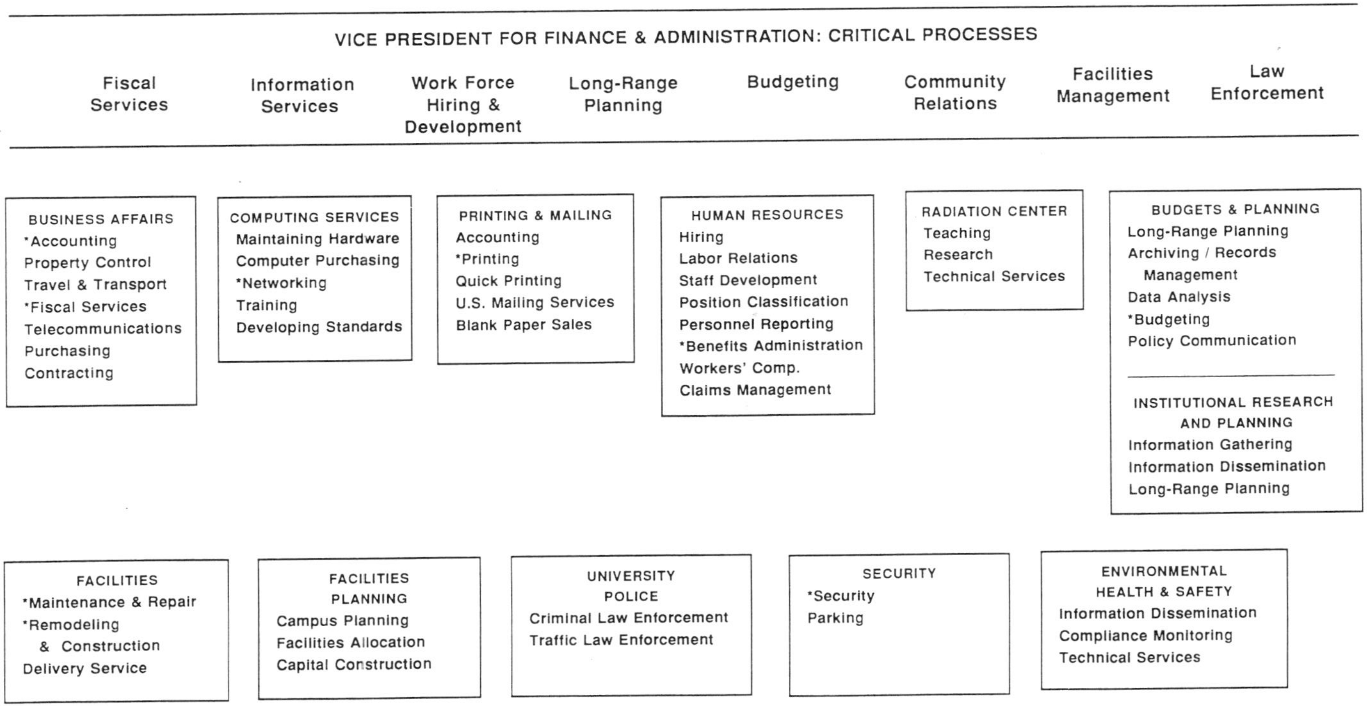

VICE PRESIDENT FOR FINANCE & ADMINISTRATION: CRITICAL PROCESSES

| Fiscal Services | Information Services | Work Force Hiring & Development | Long-Range Planning | Budgeting | Community Relations | Facilities Management | Law Enforcement |

BUSINESS AFFAIRS
•Accounting
Property Control
Travel & Transport
•Fiscal Services
Telecommunications
Purchasing
Contracting

COMPUTING SERVICES
Maintaining Hardware
Computer Purchasing
•Networking
Training
Developing Standards

PRINTING & MAILING
Accounting
•Printing
Quick Printing
U.S. Mailing Services
Blank Paper Sales

HUMAN RESOURCES
Hiring
Labor Relations
Staff Development
Position Classification
Personnel Reporting
•Benefits Administration
Workers' Comp.
Claims Management

RADIATION CENTER
Teaching
Research
Technical Services

BUDGETS & PLANNING
Long-Range Planning
Archiving / Records Management
Data Analysis
•Budgeting
Policy Communication

INSTITUTIONAL RESEARCH AND PLANNING
Information Gathering
Information Dissemination
Long-Range Planning

FACILITIES PLANNING
Campus Planning
Facilities Allocation
Capital Construction

UNIVERSITY POLICE
Criminal Law Enforcement
Traffic Law Enforcement

SECURITY
•Security
Parking

ENVIRONMENTAL HEALTH & SAFETY
Information Dissemination
Compliance Monitoring
Technical Services

FACILITIES
•Maintenance & Repair
•Remodeling & Construction
Delivery Service

•Denotes pilot team

Table 5.1. Pilot TQM Teams in Finance and Administration

Team	Division	Critical Process	Issue Statement
1A	Physical Plant	Facilities management	Reduce the amount of time it takes to complete the remodeling process.
1B	Physical Plant	Facilities management	Improve servicing of fixed equipment.
2	Printing and Mailing	Information services	Reduce the amount of time in the prepress stage of the printing process.
3	Budgets and Planning	Budgeting	Increase the timeliness of the budget-status-at-a-glance report development process.
4	Computing Services	Information services	Increase the timeliness and consistent delivery of network information.
5A	Business Affairs	Fiscal services	Decrease the number of errors in departmental journal vouchers by creating a checklist of common errors.
5B	Business Affairs	Fiscal services	Reduce the time expended in processing grant and contract documents within Business Affairs.
6	Public Safety	Safety	Decrease response time on requests for service.
7	Radiation Center	President's critical processes: teaching, research, service delivery	Increase customer demand for the center's products and streamline response process.
8	Human Resources	Work force hiring and development	Increase the speed of initial response in the information dissemination process.

8. The data are analyzed and shown in charts and graphs.
9. Solutions to the problems are developed by brainstorming. Each solution is measured against criteria that reflect customer needs. The best solutions are then implemented and their performance monitored, and they are adopted if they work.
10. If the problem is solved, fixes are standardized as normal operating procedure.

The following section analyzes experiences and results from the first ten TQM teams at OSU. The teams were created in early 1990 and worked with varying time lines. These study data were collected during the summer of 1990, when the ten teams were at various points in the TQM process.

Physical Plant Team A

The problem was to decrease the time from start to finish to complete a remodeling project. This team, formed as a pilot early in OSU's TQM imple-

Figure 5.2. Ten-Step TQM Problem-Solving Model

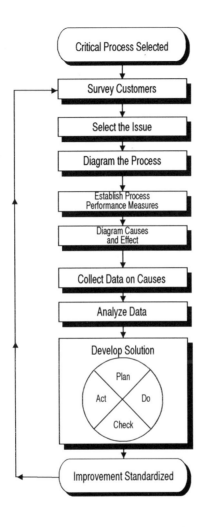

mentation, has worked through two phases of problem solving on the remodeling issue.

Phase 1. The team's first process flowchart uncovered thirty-three causes of overlaps, delays, and unnecessary paper flow. Their first TQM study led to many immediate process "cleanups" and five major changes.

Solutions. (1) The Customer Service Center was formed. Customers can call a single unit to get information about the status of a project. (2) To improve communication with customers, the team recommended and management established the position of construction superintendent. Shop supervisors report work progress to the superintendent, and customers can talk about their needs with one person, face to face. (3) Three time-saving changes suggested by subteams were implemented: hand-carrying of design and project authorization forms to the customer for consultation and completion, identification of equipment and materials that can be purchased during the design process, and a "shop participation walk-through" at the beginning of design to get input from the shops and identify possible problems.

The first set of solutions shortened the process by an average of 10 percent and reduced the flowchart to one page. A survey of customers showed that even when the completion time for a project did not decrease, they were more satisfied and more understanding of delays. They saw that the physical plant unit was concerned and working on its problems.

Phase 2. In the second phase of their TQM study, team members worked on solutions to remodeling time delays that were not addressed during phase 1.

Solutions. Because remodeling is a complex process, the team formed subteams at various times to address specific problems. Four subteam proposals are currently being tested or are now under consideration for implementation: creation of a TQM cross-functional team to address campus vehicle access problems that slow delivery of construction materials; a new "field change order" that allows on-site customer approval of proposed construction changes, ending time-consuming approval loops; a seven-step "design checklist" for consultants, aimed at eliminating design flaws that slow construction projects; and creation of a TQM cross-functional team with the Department of Purchasing to address delays in materials acquisition.

The team's solutions during its two phases of activity resulted in a total reduction of 23 percent in the average duration of the remodeling process. A customer in the Department of Mathematics said she got quick, courteous correction of a physical plant billing mistake. "The person who called me back was very concerned that we be well taken care of." Another customer, impressed with an immediate personal contact for a heating problem, said, "That's never happened before!"

Team responses were also favorable: "When we started the team, we had a roomful of individuals from various sections who were saying, 'I'm going to protect my own area.' After about three months, the walls were coming down, and now we're functioning as a team." "I think the TQM philosophy is going to prevail. People see that there are ways to change things and that they do have a voice in the process. We have changed attitudes."

Physical Plant Team B

The problem was to improve servicing of fixed equipment. OSU's fixed equipment problem began when higher education budget cuts in the early 1980s forced the physical plant to stop funding maintenance of most installed furniture and equipment. The shift of responsibility hurt both departmental budgets and the plant's relationship with its customers. In 1990, a users committee and an independent evaluation strongly recommended that the physical plant find a way to resume responsibility for servicing fixed equipment.

Because they were asked to deal with a specific problem rather than a process, the team chose to use an abbreviated TQM procedure. They began with a customer survey and found that the primary customer issues were funding of fixed equipment services and a lack of knowledge about fixed equipment.

Solution. To develop a solution to the problem, the team inventoried and established five categories of fixed equipment that could be explained to customers; estimated the costs of preventive maintenance, repair, and replacement for each category; developed a plan making the physical plant responsible for service calls and preventive maintenance, funding repairs 65 percent from physical plant and 35 percent from the department, and making the department responsible for replacement costs; and identified possible sources of physical plant funding for the plan. The team's solution decreases the responsibility of departments for costs of maintenance, service, repair, and replacement of fixed equipment by 31 percent.

Team responses were generally positive: "The best thing that came out of the team process was the concept of making the customer a partner, working out a division of responsibility in sharing the costs. That wasn't an outcome I had foreseen. It genuinely came out of the workings of the team." "I was impressed with the process. I think it is needed in physical plant as an ongoing way to solve problems. On the team I learned some things about budgeting and management and cleared up some questions. I have reservations about how our solution will be implemented."

Printing and Mailing Team

The problem was to reduce the amount of time in the prepress stage of the printing process.

Causes. Data collected on the causes of lost time in the prepress process told the team that the major problems were as follows: Customers held proofs too long, and employees were not cross-trained to help deal with absences or high work load.

Solutions. The team developed a list of solutions. In the area of customer education, the team is developing a "capabilities brochure" to show customers what printing can do for them in a realistic time frame at a reasonable cost; tours, first for internal and then for external customers, to help them understand the publication process; and seminars to teach customers how to use printing's capabilities to meet their needs. In the area of internal improvements, the team is testing time-saving steps in the intake and service request forms, a new cover sheet and policy to shorten delays through improved tracking of proofs held by customers, the position of production coordinator to negotiate and enforce job due dates, and brief daily meetings of production managers to coordinate jobs. The team's solutions are addressing each cause of lost time in the prepress process, and they project a 50 percent reduction in the number of lost days.

Team responses were positive: "One benefit I am seeing is management's cooperation in listening to employees. There is more communication. And there's a growth in teamwork. People are starting to think, 'When I do something, who else down the line will be affected?' That's a positive thing." "I really believe in the TQM process. It's just a matter of doing it and keeping on top of it. Now that we see that management is implementing our solutions, the team is enthusiastic."

Budgets and Planning Team

The problem was defined as increasing the timeliness of the budget-status-at-a-glance report development process. The team's focus was a monthly OSU budget report given to the president and vice presidents. A survey of these customers showed that timeliness was only one of their needs. Their requests were as follows: Add a report overview with a summary and analysis, add comments giving the Budgets and Planning Office perspective, distribute the report in advance of cabinet meetings, send the report to deans of colleges, improve the report's format to highlight budget problems, improve accuracy, and improve timeliness.

In the next month's report, the team immediately implemented the requested distribution and format improvements and added an overview. They then applied the remaining TQM steps to the timeliness issue.

Causes. A flowchart of the report process showed these causes of time delays: time lost in the office getting the report data from data services to the persons who needed the information; days spent reentering and recalculating other personnel expense (OPE) data, which data services calculated in a way not usable in the report; and a series of review loops that slow final approval of the report.

Solutions. (1) Rewrite the data services computer program to calculate OPE data in the form needed for the budget report. (2) Change office procedures to speed distribution of report data. (3) Implement requested report improvements to shorten approval loops. Results of solutions will not be available until distribution of the budget-status-at-a-glance report begins again in January 1994. The present ten-day preparation process should be cut in half.

Team responses focused considerable attention on the TQM process in solving problems: "TQM forces a team to go through a detailed, logical process. It encourages teamwork. For our office it was a first step toward trying a team approach, and it worked out well." "TQM will be great if they let the people below management level come up with the problems and use the process where it can be most productive." "TQM encourages people to think and work collectively in the interest of goals beyond individual performance. It enhances the organization's efficiency." "It was good to see people displaying creativity and analytical abilities that I hadn't seen them demonstrate before."

Computing Services Team

The problem initially was defined as decreasing the amount of time required for network installation. But after team members had identified and surveyed their customers, they found that this issue was not the issue of primary concern to customers. They then redefined their problem as increasing the quality of network information. Their final problem statement narrowed the issue to tracking timeliness and consistency of information delivery.

Causes. Tracking of requests for network information pinpointed the chief causes for slow or inconsistent delivery: lack of resources (staff and funds), customers' lack of basic knowledge, university computing services staff's lack of necessary information, no consistent way of dealing with requests, and lack of unit-internal communication. The team's sponsor, the computing services director, refused to accept "lack of resources" as a valid cause of information delivery problems, since the OSU administration required that any TQM team solution meet the criterion that no new money or full-time equivalents be required.

Solutions. The team continued their study and proposed ten solutions: Implement an easy-to-use, menu-driven on-line system to distribute up-to-date network information; develop short handouts for frequently requested information; place more emphasis on networking in the computing services newsletter; designate one person responsible for managing network information; direct initial network information inquiries to consultants; develop a policy and procedure for dealing with network information requests; designate a project manager for network installations; maintain familiarity with new network products and technology; implement a network training program for university computing services staff; and reorganize to implement some of the solutions. Some solutions were implemented immediately, whereas others were held for a planned departmental reorganization.

The team's response was summarized as follows: "I was interested in the TQM process at first because it has structure and method, and that was appealing to me. We found out that the process is tougher to apply to a problem than it seemed. The team had a mixed reaction to their TQM experience."

Business Affairs Team A

The problem was to decrease the number of erroneous journal vouchers (JVs) returned to departments.

Causes. When the team began measuring JV errors, they found a one-month total of 200 out of 7,971 processed, a rate of 3 percent. Of these, more than half, 103, were returned to the originating department for correction, a time-wasting process loop.

Solutions. The team tested two solutions: Based on a better understanding of what customers wanted, the JV specialist called departments and corrected most errors over the phone; and to help departments complete their JVs correctly at the outset, the specialist prepared a checklist based on data about common customer errors and sent it to all departments. The team helped her with suggestions and reviews. The JV error rate dropped from 3 percent to 2 percent, and the number of JVs returned to departments dropped dramatically, from 103 to 4. Departments told the Accounts Payable Office that they were happy to save the time it took to correct JVs themselves. Many customers called to say that they appreciated the checklist.

At the beginning, the team bogged down because their issue was too large. It would have required them to study the entire general ledger statement process. According to the team's sponsor, "TQM works best if you take problems in little chunks. . . . As soon as we narrowed the issue to the journal voucher process, we started to move."

Business Affairs Team B

The goal was to reduce the time expended in processing grant and contract documents within the Business Affairs Office.

Causes. A flowchart of the grant and contract process pinpointed time-wasting loops. Some causes of delays were waits for signatures of authorities outside OSU, loops for amendment of incorrect contract award language, routing of awards for review and signatures within OSU, and time spent hunting for account files being used by another person.

Solutions. The team proposed three main solutions: Work with the Research Office to communicate correct contract award language to researchers; develop, test, and implement a locator system for account files; and immediately implement five time-saving changes in office procedures. In addition, team data documenting delays in outside signature loops led managers to obtain agreement from the Office of the Chancellor to eliminate one loop. Also, the team recommended that a cross-functional team study a review loop within the College of Agriculture. Elimination of one outside signature loop reduced average processing days for Agricultural Research Foundation contracts from 12.7 days to 0.3 days. Although staff changes and startup of a new data base caused some "peaks," average processing days stayed within upper and lower control limits and began to move down, initially by 10 percent.

Team responses focused on the analytical tools used to reach solutions: "The flowchart was most helpful. It identified loops and made us ask, 'Why do we do this?' We need to chart many of our systems. Brainstorming causes of problems is another important element in the TQM process. Sharing information and feeding off each other's ideas gets people involved and excited." "The tools we were given opened our eyes to things we didn't think of before." "I'm kind of fired up. I think this is the way to go."

The team was frustrated at first because many causes of problems with their process were out of their control. However, they found that, supported with data, they could alert people in authority and motivate them to push for change.

Public Safety Team

The problem was defined as improving the timeliness of the security delivery process. Surveys showed that customers most wanted more frequent building security checks.

Causes. The team's data gathering pinpointed a major cause of building security problems: The five officers who make regular security checks on two hundred campus buildings were spending almost one-fourth of their time giving motorist, medical, and other general assists to students, staff, and campus visitors.

Solutions. (1) The university police and motor pool departments were asked, and they agreed, to share responsibility for providing assists, freeing the security officers for more frequent building checks. A university police officer joined the team to work out implementation. (2) A laser barcode reader was placed on the exterior doors of buildings to reduce paperwork during building checks. (3) The number of medical assists provided by security officers was reduced by revising the assist policy. The number of daily building security checks averaged 824 for August, September, and October of 1990, up from 584 in July, just before the team's solutions were implemented.

Typical team responses were as follows: "For me the increased communication between police and security was the biggest positive improvement from TQM. I've enjoyed being a member of the TQM team. It's good to work with a group that really accomplishes things." "The changes we made should cut down on thefts and, in the long run, save money for the university and the state."

Radiation Center Team

The Radiation Center sought to increase customer demand for its research and service capabilities and to streamline the response process. Early in 1990, the center identified its customer groups and conducted a survey. Responses showed the need for several process improvements and new services.

Phase 1. Solutions implemented to meet customer needs were installation of a new irradiation facility in the reactor; addition of a service to calibrate radiation detection instruments for OSU researchers and Oregon state agencies; addition of a radon-monitoring service for OSU and other state institutions; implementation of a slide and video presentation designed to show OSU and other potential customers how the Radiation Center could help them; elimination of delays in shipping irradiated samples by improving the sample-tracking system; and addition of a new 7,000-curie cobalt 60 gamma irradiator.

Phase 2. The TQM team chose to focus on improving the efficiency of a basic Radiation Center activity, the instrumental neutron activation analysis (INAA) process. The team measured the cost efficiency of the INAA process by checking the qualifications of staff performing each INAA function. A process flowchart and a fish-bone diagram identified a primary cause of excess costs: Some tasks were being carried out by a person more highly qualified than necessary. Elimination of this cost inefficiency would also increase the time available for development of new techniques and improvement of other research and service processes. The Radiation Center team is currently collecting data on this cause and will develop solutions to improve the INAA process.

Human Resources Team

A survey and a two-week collection of telephone-solicited data told the team that their OSU customers needed quick, human responses to phoned-in questions, and that the customers were receiving this kind of service only 58 percent of the time. The problem was to increase speed of initial response in the information dissemination process.

Cause. As they worked through the TQM study process, the team, using their data, pinpointed the chief cause of the shunting of callers from human to automated answering. Staff members were busy on other calls or working with walk-in customers.

Solutions. (1) Change telephone configuration by adding lines and another telephone; extend the number of rings before a caller receives a message, giving employees longer to catch a call; and send a busy signal rather than a message when the human resources manager is on the telephone to let callers know she is in. (2) Establish office telephone policies to change telephone messages each day or whenever staff are out of the office for four hours or more; set telephones to go directly to message whenever staff member is away from the desk; and return all calls within four hours. (3) Cut the number of calls by giving customers needed information: print an often-requested agency number on a form; stock departments with three common forms; send out posters of key human resources telephone numbers; and encourage use of e-mail.

Calls answered by a person on a first try increased to 67 percent in August, nearing the team's goal of 75 percent. October 1990 data indicated an increase to 81 percent. Significantly, a person who acts as a human resources telephone backup said, "Before we implemented solutions, I spent 35 percent of my time taking benefits calls. Now that is down to 1 percent."

At the end of their study, the team members reported to OSU's president and the finance and administration vice president and directors. Asked if they would recommend TQM, the team gave a unanimous yes. "We thought we knew what our problems were. TQM helped us find out what they really were. TQM has given us a process to use in the future."

Customer Survey

It is important to verify perceptions of improved services with those receiving the services as well as with those providing them.

Evaluating OSU's TQM Pilot Program. Following TQM principles, the program "customers"—the team members, leaders, and facilitators who had participated in the pilot program—were surveyed. These were the people who were closest to OSU's TQM process. Their responses would be used to improve it.

The survey was conducted and a report prepared by an impartial outside consultant, Joann DeMott. She used a written survey tool to obtain participants' opinions. Its three sections were designed to collect information about team participants' perceptions of their ability to apply TQM problem-solving tools and techniques, participants' preferences in TQM training, and participants' evaluations of the results of the initial TQM implementation and training, based on success criteria identified by team leaders and facilitators as the ideal TQM implementation. The written survey was followed by a series of personal interviews to elicit more in-depth information from at least one member of each team.

Summary of Survey Results. The overall effect of TQM appeared to be positive in the opinion of 63 percent of the team members who responded and of 72 percent of the leaders and facilitators. Around 66 percent of the team members believed that the examination of work processes and teamwork had increased staff knowledge and increased communication within their departments. Evidently, the work of a few positively affected the many.

Among leaders and facilitators, 72 percent agreed that employee morale had increased as a result of the pilot teams. Team members were not so sure, 45 percent believing that morale remained at the same level as before.

Some results of the survey were affected by the fact that many teams had not yet completed their TQM projects. For instance, 58 percent of the team members and 82 percent of the facilitators and leaders who responded did not know whether their respective customers were satisfied with the changes that the teams made. Teams were encouraged to obtain feedback from customers after their solutions were implemented.

Similarly, about one-half of the respondents did not yet know whether waste of time, materials, or energy had been reduced in their processes. Only one-quarter believed that work quality had improved through increased staff satisfaction.

· As a noteworthy contrast, 50 percent of the team members believed that they had seen "visible support of top management" for their TQM work, and 82 percent of the facilitators and leaders believed they had not seen it. Team members evidently felt more support than did their leaders from department heads and top-level people. They said that visits to their team meetings by the vice president for finance and administration and other administrators were "very helpful and very welcome."

One survey item received a consistent response from everyone: 84 percent of the team members and 82 percent of the leaders and facilitators disagreed with the statement "Duties have been removed from my work load to attend team meetings." The fact that sponsors and supervisors expected TQM responsibilities to be added to the work load created difficulties for many staff members. Among the many comments on this issue were the following: "Having to add TQM to other job duties [was a problem]. We welcomed the chance to have the team so we could take the time to change processes we knew needed changing, but it was hard to set other work aside." "[It was hard to] find time to devote to team efforts between meetings. Although the sponsor assured us that this was important and we should make it a priority, the pressure comes from the customers, and our work load was not really reduced." "The process is very time-consuming, especially for the team leader. There was no release time either for training or TQM team meetings." Obviously, participants saw the time commitment required for TQM training meetings and preparation as a problem.

Statements About TQM Implementation. Following are some of the statements about TQM that showed the greatest agreement among team participants: 82 percent of the team members believed that the team leader did not dominate but served as an equal team member, and that the leader was prepared and involved. 79 percent of members and 94 percent of leaders and facilitators believed that team manuals were important and should continue to be given to all team members. 79 percent of members and 88 percent of leaders and facilitators believed that team members should have the right to leave the team if they so desire. 74 percent of members and 88 percent of leaders and facilitators believed that surveying their customers was an important and telling experience and that meeting away from the regular work area was important. 71 percent of members agreed that teams should be formed at all levels of finance and administration to improve processes. 66 percent of members believed that the weekly team meetings seriously interrupted their ability to get their work done.

Among leaders and facilitators, 82 percent believed that the confidentiality that was one of the team ground rules led to secrecy, which affected communications in their departments; 76 percent believed that facilitators did not receive adequate training on how to facilitate before the teams began, though 71 percent believed that the role and responsibilities of the facilitator were clear; 76 percent believed that the role and responsibilities of the leader were clear; and 71 percent believed that it would have been better if sponsors had received the TQM team training before the pilot teams.

Clearly, dissemination of more information is needed. At the end of the pilot program, between 76 and 88 percent of the team participants were still not sure why OSU had decided to implement TQM. To illustrate, one team member raised the question at a meeting: "I don't understand why we're doing TQM. What have we done wrong?"

Some staff members evidently see TQM as a punishment for not meeting some unknown expectations rather than as a way to move forward. One possible remedy is to give employees an introductory videotape and a published philosophical statement about why TQM is being implemented at OSU and its benefits over time.

Surveying of customers is very important. Although it is a time-consuming part of the problem-solving process, direct contact with individuals who receive products or services is well worth the effort. One team member said, "Things will never be the same for me. I now know these people who get my products. . . . On our team, we learned lots of things that need to be changed . . . lots of things we didn't know about."

Insights from Personal Interviews. At least one representative from each team was interviewed by the consultant. During the individual interviews, representatives made observations and suggestions for improvements that may prove helpful.

"Consider your problem-solving experiences before and after your team's training. Do you believe you are less or more effective in solving problems in general or on a work team?"

Most of those interviewed believed they and their fellow team members had increased their problem-solving skills as a result of the TQM pilot team. Only three representatives did not feel that they had personally improved their skills; these individuals were seasoned team members with experience on teams outside of OSU. It is important to note that for three-quarters of the representatives interviewed, the TQM team experience had been their first.

Training of new team members on how to work together, therefore, should be of great importance to OSU.

In the best cases, team members became more familiar with one another as professionals, which helped reduce adversarial relationships. According to one person interviewed, individual interest had to be melded into the group interest, which resulted in more give-and-take. Communication among team members increased as they learned more about the chosen process within their department.

TQM was seen as an excellent tool for organizing thoughts; focusing on specifics of a problem; finding the root cause of, rather than simply talking about, the symptoms; and developing solutions. Most of those interviewed appreciated the structured framework of the problem-solving methodology and felt that it significantly contributed to a more effective, coordinated team effort.

In the worst cases, teams found it hard to keep moving on their problems when the group could not focus on a specific issue. In one case, the purpose of the team changed midstream.

"Consider your trainer. Were you satisfied with the trainer's knowledge and style? At what were you delighted? What could be improved?"

The pilot teams were served by one of two trainers. One individual is a professional trainer employed with OSU's Department of Human Resources; the other is an outside professional TQM consultant and trainer. The trainers created the teams and stayed with them through most of the problem-solving process. However, in order to discourage dependence, trainers were phased out of the problem-solving process as the teams progressed. Responsibilities for teaching the TQM tools were then assumed by each team facilitator. With only one team did the trainer remain through the entire problem-solving process.

In the best cases, the team representatives were very happy with their trainer's level of knowledge and style of delivery. Since the information was new to most, they had to trust the trainers, and most felt confident in the overall knowledge base of the trainers. Two comments represent the team members who were most pleased: "I appreciated the skill of our trainer to make things understood. I liked the simple, down-to-earth approach used to explain things." "Our team really enjoyed and benefited from our trainer's enthusiasm for TQM."

Most often, trainers were complimented by representatives for encouraging team members to open up and make contributions to the teams. The trainers were seen as having done a good job of holding things together and keeping the groups on track. "We would have faltered without our trainer," one interviewee reported.

In the worst cases, interviewees did not believe that they had received enough training on the tools of the problem-solving process. Having received only a quick overview of the process, they would question the trainer's depth of knowledge of TQM. In one case, the trainer's knowledge of statistics and experience in solving business problems were questioned. The interviewee suggested that more information about the trainer's background and experience with TQM would have instilled more immediate confidence. In two cases, the trainer was perceived as having been interested in other teams more than the team at hand and only interested in saving money, not improving the process in other ways. In two cases, the trainers were perceived as having left the teams before the teams were ready.

"What improvements would you recommend for the training of others in TQM?"

Representatives were generally happy with the just-in-time training approach, although they would have appreciated a full university example showing the use of all of the quality-control tools and techniques. The design of working in teams to solve real, day-to-day problems was seen by most as effective. There was agreement that the problem-solving process has to be experienced to be thoroughly understood. In the words of one representative, "TQM has to be experienced . . . like swimming. You just have to get in the water and do it!"

The representatives interviewed had mixed beliefs about the usefulness of the team manual. Some thought it was helpful as a future resource, even though there was very little narrative to explain the concepts on the pages; others thought it was a waste of paper because the material was covered verbally in the team training; one representative had not received a manual at all.

Most representatives agreed that weekly team meetings were productive and necessary to complete the problem-solving process in a reasonable amount of time. Some felt that the meetings should have been held more often at the beginning of the process to learn about TQM and focus on the issue; then they should have met less frequently as the team progressed. Others felt that interruptions of the meeting schedules when trainers were unavailable to meet with the teams hurt the teams' effectiveness.

Several teams began the problem-solving process by meeting three hours each week; then, over the course of the process, they reduced the duration of the meetings to about one and one-half to two hours. This seemed to work well for these teams. Half of the representatives believed that three-hour meetings were good if the team members were moving forward and if they were not confined to a small, stuffy room. Four-hour meetings would be too long, in their opinion, except at the beginning when teams were being introduced to the TQM concepts, vocabulary, and problem-solving overview. Meetings lasting for one and one-half hours seemed best once the team members were used to working together and knew what they were to do in the process.

"What other comments would you offer?"

At the completion of the interview, representatives were given an opportunity to offer general comments about their experiences and observations during the pilot project. In the best cases, representatives were very positive about their experiences on the pilot teams. They especially enjoyed interviewing their external customers, making the process flowcharts, and completing the fish-bone diagrams. They liked the concept of passing their respective products or services on to internal customers, their co-workers. In the words of one representative, "Now I want to make the next guy's job easier."

The representatives were very interested in seeing cross-departmental teams formed. One person stated that it was difficult when one department was implementing TQM while another department, with a different vice president, had not yet started the process. This difference presented difficulties when the work process under consideration was shared between these two departments. The pilot team could only improve the part of the process that they owned rather than look at the process as a whole. The situation will be improved as everyone at OSU becomes familiar with TQM and can use the tools and problem-solving process together.

In the worst cases, leaders were seen as unwilling to allow their teams to make specific recommendations for fear of not satisfying a sponsor or administrator. Several representatives suggested that teams should proceed, making their recommendations based on their data analyses and best judgments; then, if a sponsor could not accept the recommendations, he or she would work with the team, either personally or in writing, to develop an acceptable solution.

In one case, team members were reportedly angry when, in examining the problems of their chosen work process, they discovered information that they believed had been hidden from them. The information proved important enough to turn the team in a new and positive direction toward developing the solution. In the words of one representative, "You learn things while investigating a problem. People have to be able to talk to each other . . . at all levels . . . without retribution."

Representatives were aware of the stresses on their managers in moving from the old way of managing to the new way, but they were hopeful. As one representative stated, "We need to be aware of the potential for misuse of TQM. But we all have to drive out fear and trust the process."

Directors' Cross-Functional Team

In response to this customer evaluation of OSU's pilot program, the vice president for finance and administration formed a cross-functional team to improve the process used to implement TQM. The team, made up of the unit's directors, met weekly, with the vice president as team leader and the staff development officer as facilitator.

The team constructed a flowchart of the TQM implementation process used at OSU, then used data from the evaluation survey to identify causes of implementation problems. To complete the next step in the TQM problem-solving process, the team brainstormed a list of twenty possible solutions, including those identified in the customer survey. They collapsed and reduced the list, then developed the following criteria for testing each solution: measurably reduce implementation time, improve the issue process, address an identified customer need, and achieve results with a reasonable expenditure of time and resources.

The team developed the following solutions, which will be tried as finance and administration units continue to establish TQM study teams: (1) Let the sponsor determine whether the team will address a critical process or a specific problem, but have the team develop the issue statement and then rebalance its membership to include owners of the process to be studied. (2) Base team study on issue statements that are concise, quantifiable, and related to a critical process. (3) Create a new type of team, the problem-solving team, to respond quickly to a major crisis, using an abbreviated TQM process to reach an immediate solution. (4) To support the team and publicize TQM, print reports on the issues and results of team study in the staff newsletter. (5) Develop a new, longer, and more comprehensive training curriculum for team leaders and facilitators. (6) Develop a new OSU TQM training manual, using real OSU examples. (7) Develop a matrix to coordinate scheduling of teams, training, and facilitator assignments. The logarithmic growth in numbers of teams requires close attention to organizational details. (8) Include team building in TQM training. (9) Integrate just-in-time team skills training into the TQM process when teamwork issues arise.

Conclusion and Recommendations

While TQM is a relatively simple concept, putting it to work in a university is more challenging than many of us at OSU anticipated. The language was foreign to us (universities use words different from those in industry). The teamwork approach to problem solving was unfamiliar to most of our midlevel managers. But so far, we consider TQM a success at OSU. We now have twenty teams operating, and the results have been impressive. Time has been saved, costs have been reduced, people have been empowered at all levels, and morale has improved.

Managers must lead the TQM process. Each manager's job is to demonstrate continually, both in words and in action, that TQM is a top priority. This means regularly using study teams, reviewing progress in staff meetings, providing training to everyone, and recognizing and rewarding those who use the process.

Let me conclude by enumerating seven key points learned from our pilot program.

• Waste in our processes was reduced or eliminated. All ten pilot teams were able to show significant improvement in their processes. In most cases, this resulted in savings of time, material, and cost. Work quality was improved through a more satisfied staff.

• Recommendations made by teams were implemented. The most important single measure of success for team members was the implementation of their recommended changes. It is critical for sponsors to work closely with teams as they go through the process and identify criteria that will make all of the solutions workable. To date, 80 percent of the teams' recommendations have been implemented.

• The customers of our processes were satisfied with the changes made. Feedback from customers is important! Feedback helps to ensure that customers are aware of the improvements made to the process, allows for corrections if more improvement is still needed, and helps reward the team. Customer delight is a very satisfying reward and a powerful motivator.

• TQM increased problem-solving skills. For three quarters of the team members, this was their first formal training in developing team-building and problem-solving skills.

• The addition of TQM to other job duties was a problem. Everyone welcomed the chance to have a team so they could take the time to change processes that they knew needed changing, but it was hard to set other work aside. Some help should be provided, if possible, to lighten work loads.

• Visible support from top management is essential. Attendance by senior management at training and team meetings is very helpful. There also needs to be a published philosophical statement about why TQM is being implemented, how TQM can help the institution realize its vision, and the benefits of TQM over time.

• As a result of the work of the pilot teams, employee morale was increased. Seventy-two percent of team leaders and facilitators believe employee morale has increased. A staff survey was conducted before TQM started, and staff will be surveyed in the spring of 1994 to reconfirm this belief.

One team member's words, cited in the evaluation survey, expressed the hopes of many in this way: "I've been at OSU for nearly ten years, and I've experienced a lot of stumbling blocks to getting things done. I had pretty much decided that I was just going to come to work, do my job, and not make waves. I got into a rut, and I didn't see much hope. Now TQM has opened another door, and I see a chance to make some changes that just make common sense. Total Quality Management seems to be OSU's answer!"

L. EDWIN COATE is vice chancellor of business and administrative services at the University of California, Santa Cruz. He was vice president for finance and administration at Oregon State University.

Financial management in higher education has been improved markedly over the past twenty-five years by analyses focused on revenue production and several dimensions of costs.

Multidimensional Analyses and Cost-Revenue Relationships

William E. Vandament

As fiscal management in American higher education has matured in the past twenty-five years, increased attention has been paid to four basic factors: (1) the behavior of costs, that is, the manner in which fixed and variable factors contribute separately to direct or unit costs; (2) analyses of cost-revenue relationships to augment an earlier emphasis on cost factors in isolation from revenues; (3) the differing effects of one-time and recurring costs and revenues; and (4) analyses directed toward the use of a variety of funding sources to support core general fund activities. In part, this growing sophistication in financial management can be viewed as a response to the serious financial difficulties of the 1970s and early 1980s that were brought on by economic recession and declines in the number of college-age students. During that period many institutions became convinced that they could not merely make short-term adjustments and wait for the financial clouds to lift; they were forced to take long-term actions that involved more than deferring expenditures or achieving cost reductions in existing programs. These actions required that financial managers develop multidimensional analytical tools to identify potential cost savings and additional revenues to support programs that were threatened.

Cost-Revenue Relationships

Financial management in higher education, and, indeed, in most nonprofit or public organizations, traditionally focused on providing stewardship for funds derived from a limited number of sources, usually tuition and government appropriations. For all practical purposes, this focus translated to an overriding concern about containing costs and justifying appropriation levels; financial planning was largely restricted to budgeting activity centered on the distribution of whatever revenues were received from those sources, over which the institution was presumed to have little control.

As financial management in American public institutions evolved during the 1960s, analytical tools were developed to measure and compare unit costs in institutions and academic disciplines. These analyses—often expressed as the average cost per credit hour or full-time-equivalent student—were used to identify high-cost programs and to establish guidelines for the allocation of funds among and within institutions. Comparisons of costs within and between institutional programs received widespread attention, particularly in public institutions, as states attempted to achieve equity and productivity for the several colleges and universities competing for limited state resources. Often, these unit-cost studies provided the information from which funding formulas, usually expressed as appropriation-per-student, were developed.

A subsequent focus on the separate fixed and variable cost components of unit costs emerged in the late 1970s and set the stage for the greater attention that is now given to the revenue implications of financial decisions. It became clear with the segregation of these two cost factors that while pricing—or appropriation—strategies were generally based on unit measures (for example, dollars per credit hour), the unit costs of providing these services varied greatly, depending on the volume or enrollment levels of the courses offered. In short, the marginal costs of adding five students to an existing course were far less than establishing a course for the first five students. Clearly, the financial implications of decisions now had to take into account the interaction of the volume of activity with fixed and variable costs and unit-pricing factors.

Fixed and Variable Costs. As enrollment declines were encountered in many colleges and universities during the late 1970s, the fact that the institutions' costs contained fixed components, as well as those that varied with enrollments, became painfully clear. Administrators struggled with cuts disproportionately made to direct services because some of the overhead costs of supporting programs remained nearly constant despite the reduced volume of direct program activity. It was often discovered that an untouchable administrative structure had to remain essentially intact, that a core set of underutilized laboratories and equipment had to be maintained, and that sparsely enrolled courses had to be offered if the institution was to meet its program commitments. External critics noted wryly at the time that university financial managers had been content with funding formulas based on simple unit-cost measures during periods of enrollment growth and that they discovered their inadequacies only when enrollment increases had been replaced by declines and threats of proportional losses in funding.

Nevertheless, a flurry of analyses marked by the separation of costs into fixed and variable components emerged under the auspices of the National Association of College and University Business Officers (for example, National Association of College and University Business Officers, 1980). The term *cost behavior analysis*, developed by Robinson, Ray, and Turk (1977) at Peat, Marwick and Mitchell, appeared frequently in the literature and in practice. The cost behavior analyses were useful in predicting the cost impacts of increasing or decreasing the volume in a number of instructional and administrative activities.

Revenues as Well as Costs. On the revenue side, it became apparent in reducing the scale of programs that institutions had to "discount" their savings to reflect losses in revenue formerly derived from lost tuition and state support that was tied by formula to enrollment, or volume. Sometimes the revenue losses exceeded the actual cost savings that were obtained by reducing the volume of services. In short, the importance of the cost-revenue relationships of programs targeted for elimination or reduction in scale was highlighted.

Increasingly complex financial analyses of relationships between cost, income, and volume have emerged in which direct costs have been broken into separate fixed and variable components and unit-cost measures have been relegated to the role of providing early-warning or screening information about program activities that should be examined in greater detail. These follow-up analyses are made to determine if high costs are reversible and if the volume of activity, and associated revenues, can be adjusted to produce more favorable cost-revenue relationships (see Vandament, 1989).

Fixed and Variable Costs, Volume, and Revenue Generation. Academic programs with high unit costs customarily receive considerable attention when institutions face fiscal stringency or seek to generate savings that can be reallocated to program activities of high institutional priority. In the past, efforts were often directed almost exclusively to achieving efficiency by lowering expenditures in high-cost programs to bring them more in line with the costs of other programs. Reduction in costs, where possible, should always be a goal of financial management. However, it cannot be regarded as the sole option when the goal is to lower unit costs or achieve more favorable cost-revenue relationships in expensive programs. In addressing the challenges of expensive (for example, high-unit-cost) programs, further examination must be conducted to determine whether the cost-revenue imbalance is due to high fixed or variable costs, or both, and whether these conditions are reversible. Alternatively, the programs should be assessed for additional revenue-generating capability through growth in the number of persons served, increased fees to users, or better utilization of existing capacity, or by off-loading some costs to revenue sources other than the institutional general fund. In the latter case, a general use budget, as described in a subsequent section here, may be beneficial.

High Fixed Costs and Volume. The problem of high fixed costs may resist corrective action under some circumstances but may be reversible in others. These costs, which are not related systematically to the volume of program enrollment or other activity, have in many instances been shown not to be fixed at all, that is, if one has assumed that all fixed costs are not susceptible to change. Even the costs associated with the position of institutional president, usually regarded as a necessary cost for an institution of any size, have in rare cases been adjusted when two or more institutions have merged! As institutions have restructured in response to fiscal crises, several have found that administrative structure can sometimes be downsized by combining units or by reducing the number of hierarchical steps in the administration. In the academic program, this may involve combining departments to reduce the extent to which fixed administrative costs contribute to the overall unit costs of each affected program.

In some instances, the costs of maintaining laboratory facilities have been reduced by the use of new technology. In chemistry, for example, the shift to microanalyses for instructional purposes has served to decrease both the fixed and variable components associated with the laboratory experience. The use of computerized "rats" in a few psychology departments has retained some of the hands-on educational experience while eliminating the need to maintain expensive vivarium facilities for instructional purposes. In many of the cases in which such fixed costs have been reduced, of course, the trade-off has involved the investment of one-time resources to gain recurring savings in fixed costs. But, in short, the lesson learned during the past several years has been that while fixed costs may not be directly related to volume, they are not necessarily impervious to modification.

In some situations, however, high fixed costs exist that cannot be altered if the program is to survive. It is noteworthy that in those cases in which high fixed costs are accompanied by low variable—or marginal—costs, the appropriate remedy for high unit costs and the way to gain more favorable cost-revenue relationships is growth in volume. This can be true even when such growth involves the commitment of additional recurring expenditures. Investment in the growth of a program with high unit costs can sometimes require courage because the natural tendency is to reduce the scale of such programs, to cut one's losses if the program is to be maintained at all. Uninitiated critics are likely to point out in such situations that "it doesn't make sense to increase production when you are losing money on each one you sell." Such investment does make sense, however, when the variable unit costs are lower than the unit charges paid by the new clients that are added by growth.

In fact, the strategy of reducing volume in a program with high fixed and low variable costs will result in higher unit costs and may only compound fiscal problems, because the lost revenues from downsizing may actually exceed the savings in costs. This phenomenon has long been demonstrated in basic business courses through analyses in which the break-even volume point is projected for new enterprises. In the university setting, these analyses of cost-revenue-volume relationships can provide crucial information about the effects of any downsizing that results in lowered institutional enrollment and subsequent losses in tuition, state support, or both.

The strategy of growing out of a financial problem, however, is contingent on the growth potential of the program in question, perhaps of the institution as a whole. If a potential expanded market cannot be identified for the program and fixed costs cannot be reduced sufficiently, the only alternatives open are to eliminate the program or to look elsewhere in the institution for excesses of revenue over expenditures, accepting the fact that the program in question will continue to be an institutional burden that must be maintained in the interests of protecting the institution's mission.

In summary, with regard to high fixed costs, one should start by determining whether these costs are susceptible to reduction through restructuring of the means by which services are provided. If high fixed costs are intractable, but variable costs are low and market potential is high, improvement in the cost-revenue relationship can be obtained through growth, that is, increased volume of activity. Lowering volume when there are high, intractable fixed costs and low variable costs will only result in a worse cost-revenue relationship, because the cost savings will probably be less than the revenue that is lost.

High Variable Costs. On the other hand, high intractable costs that are variable present no possibilities for improved cost-revenue relationships. In those situations in which high variable costs may be due to such factors as individualized instruction or high contact hours in supervised instruction, increases in volume may only increase the total revenue shortfall, because the variable unit costs exceed the revenues gained for each unit. In cases with inordinately high variable costs, financial relief can be obtained only by raising the price to consumers or by reducing volume and thus limiting the absolute flow of resources that are not matched by income.

Utilization of Instructional Capacity. Fixed and variable cost distinctions are appropriate at the level of the individual course or course section. Under most circumstances, nearly all of the costs associated with offering a course section can be considered fixed, and additional variable costs tied to increased volume may be negligible in many situations. The faculty member must be paid, the classroom heated and lighted if the class is provided for even a minimum number of students; the variable costs of books and other supplies are usually borne by the individual students. The work loads of faculty and adjunct instructors are customarily measured on the basis of the credit hours associated with courses assigned to the instructor over varying course enrollments. Differences in the value of these course assignments occur only under unusual circumstances, for example, if the course is a self-supporting course in which the instructor is paid on a per student basis or in the instance in which exceptional responsibilities are required, as in the teaching of very large lecture courses. Under conditions of negligible variable costs, increases in enrollment from small class size to the maximum enrollment allowed in a course can generate increased revenue with minor incremental costs. Alternately, if undersubscribed courses can serve as substitutes for students enrolled in other undersubscribed courses, one can reduce costs by eliminating courses without affecting the core services that are provided to students.

It is useful, therefore, to have measures of the instructional capacity for all of the academic departments and to compare those measures with the utilization of that capacity based on actual enrollment. The utilization statistics thus derived represent an additional step in the traditional analyses of course and section sizes that have been used to target courses for elimination, but not used to examine the other areas in which the enrollments lost through course elimination could be recaptured. The utilization measures also are useful in determining the extent to which student demand is accommodated. A department with very high utilization must be flagged for further study about increased market potential and must be analyzed to determine if students' degree progress is being adversely affected by excessively high demand in comparison to the capacity of course offerings.

A utilization study of a sample undergraduate department, Department X, is shown in Table 6.1. The course formats are assumed to be comparable (with the exception of individual study sections) to simplify the example. Department X, with ten full-time faculty members, provided eighteen courses using a standard format and ten individual study opportunities per semester. With a total capacity for 1,090 course enrollments, actual total enrollment for the semester was recorded at 753, which represents a 69 percent utilization of capacity. The courses with enrollment capacities of 15 and 30 were upper-division courses taken primarily by the department's majors. Four of the upper-division courses are required of all majors, but students are allowed some choices in selecting another four upper-division courses. Mandated to eliminate two faculty positions, Department X noted the relatively low utilization of upper-division courses and decided to eliminate some of the choices provided to majors. Because total credit hour requirements remained unchanged for majors, the elimination of some choices resulted in little loss in total upper-division enrollment and increased utilization of the diminished instructional capacity of the department. No lessening of support to a program can be achieved without negative effects; in this case, there is now less choice for student majors and increased teaching and advising effort for the faculty. However, the department was able to protect its large, popular introductory courses, which serve the institution's general education program and are effective tools for recruiting students into the department's major program.

The trade-off for increasing the percentage utilization of instructional

Table 6.1. Utilization of Capacity: Department X

Course Enrollment Limit	Number of Sections	Total Capacity	Average Total Enrollment	Average Section Size	Percentage Utilization
		Prior to Reduction of Capacity			
1	10	10	10	1	100
15	8	120	80	10	67
30	12	360	236	20	66
60	6	360	215	36	60
120	2	240	212	106	88
Total	38	1,090	753	20	69
		Following Reduction of Capacity			
1	12	12	12	1	100
15	6	90	70	12	78
30	9	270	224	25	83
60	5	300	205	41	68
120	2	240	212	106	88
Total	34	912	723	21	79

Note: Departmental faculty staffing reduced from 10 to 8 full-time members; student-faculty ratio increased from 15.1 to 18.1.

capacity is often decreased student choice. The higher the utilization of offerings, the less choice that there is available to students in selecting their programs. However, in the effective management of the college or university, it is customary to assign the highest priority to ensuring that students can make progress toward their degrees without delays caused by course unavailability; therefore, in times of fiscal constraint efforts, a desirable goal must be to maximize the use of instructional capacity in core courses of institutional programs.

Actually, one can expect to see some increased utilization as an unplanned by-product of the elimination of faculty positions. During recent years, for example, the utilization of courses offered at Northern Michigan University has climbed from 65 to 75 percent. In my opinion, utilization figures much above 75 percent will probably have an adverse impact on student degree progress unless, of course, the programs of a given university involve a major core curriculum in which few choices about courses and the times of their meeting are provided to the students. It is useful in planning for reductions, however, to make use of all information about instructional capacity and of program knowledge concerning which underutilized courses can substitute for those courses that are eliminated if the institution is to maintain its total student enrollment levels and protect its revenue base.

One-time and Recurring Considerations

Distinctions between one-time and recurring expenses and revenues have likewise received increased attention as financial managers have struggled to gain control over long-term institutional commitments. The initial motivation for maintaining one-time and recurring distinctions was related to cost control. For example, many so-called mandated cost increases from year to year were traditionally related to annualizing costs that were borne for only a partial year during the year that expenditure commitments were initially made. Midyear salary increases represent one typical situation in which the future was mortgaged by public institutions or the states that provided funding to them. In other situations, problems were created by the mismatch of recurring obligations with sources of revenue that were either nonrecurring or unstable. Again, some institutions learned the one-time versus recurring distinction the hard way when faced with the prospect of funding positions or salary increases previously supported by grant or lottery revenues that were greatly diminished from earlier levels.

To provide a clearer index of the extent to which current actions will result in future commitments, some universities supplemented traditional current-fund budgets, which delineate the disposition of funds for a given fiscal year, with recurring or base budgets; in some instances, they have shifted their primary budgeting formats to those reflecting recurring or base resources. With a significant focus now on the balance between recurring income and obligations, institutions have given increased priority to investing one-time funds to achieve either lowered expenditures or higher revenue generation on a recurring basis. Early examples of this type of investment are the many energy-saving programs in which one-time expenditures to retrofit the mechanical systems of buildings resulted in lowered annual heating or air-conditioning costs.

As the faculty and staff positions of U.S. universities have become occupied increasingly with senior, and thus higher-paid, personnel in the late 1980s and early 1990s, many universities have invested one-time funds in early retirement plans to induce voluntary separation from the university, thus generating recurring savings through replacements at junior levels. Of course, these options are available only to institutions with sufficient unrestricted fund balances available to make such up-front investments, or with the ability to borrow funds from other sources such as their state governments or endowments that can be repaid from recurring savings in future years.

Actions to invest one-time funds have underscored the importance of maintaining adequate fund balances; those balances not only serve as reserves to cover the temporary problems of cutbacks in funding or unexpected expenditures but also allow institutions the means to make one-time investments to ensure the longer-term financial health of the institutions. To many persons engaged in financial management over a long period of time, it has been gratifying to see this more active financial management in higher education. These trends mark a significant advance over the practice of mere stewardship over whatever funds were generated on a short-term basis through student tuition or government support. In short, this active approach has meant that universities increasingly are becoming more the masters of their own fates and are able to weather the vicissitudes of fluctuations in their primary income sources with fewer instances of emergency, draconian measures that sometimes threaten the institutions' futures. If nothing else, colleges and universities with adequate net worth have bought themselves time so that they can deal with crises in measured, thoughtful ways that do not undermine their ability to fulfill their missions or merely postpone future expenditures for such things as library acquisitions, equipment, and building maintenance.

Using All Resources

Although colleges and universities have during the past few decades increased the sophistication of analyses to reflect more accurately the relationships of volume to costs and revenues, and although they have increasingly differentiated one-time and recurring costs and revenues, their analyses often continue to be restricted to specific categories of funds. For example, the instructional program is largely supported by an institution's unrestricted general fund, that is, that pool of resources for which no specific purpose has been identified by the funding source. It should be noted, however, that an institution can often rely on additional funds to help support its course of programs.

In part, the neglect of some available sources of funding can be attributed to a basic characteristic of university reporting, the use of fund accounting. In fund accounting, financial records are customarily segregated into various fund groups, each having specified sources of funding and specifications on use that are defined in their acquisition. The restricted fund group contains all of those funds received from outside sources in which the donor, or granting or contracting agency, has specified that only a given set of activities will be supported by the funds in question. Most colleges and universities also have auxiliary funds in which reside the business activities of auxiliary enterprises that essentially function as freestanding businesses. Examples of auxiliary enterprises are the residence halls, bookstore, and athletics department that usually are expected to operate in a self-sufficient manner from revenues they generate through sales and services. In fund accounting, one also frequently encounters funds that have been segregated for internal management purposes, usually to ensure that portions of the university's unrestricted general funds are not diverted to some purpose that is considered secondary or extraneous to the university's primary mission. For example, academic departments may operate art museums or theatrical production companies that are expected to generate their own revenues and that are maintained separately from the unrestricted funds revenue.

The practice of fund accounting has been under fire during the past few years by board members from several leading universities who have formed a consortium of board members and fiscal officers. Their primary intent is to report financial information without regard to the various fund groups. Unfortunately, it is usually necessary to have resources and expenditures segregated into fund groups; the indiscriminate pooling of these funds obscures important information about the management of various activities and, in some instances, may be an illegal practice. With many auxiliary funds, for example, where bonds have been issued, a necessary condition of the bonding process is to ensure investors that the funds will be used for the stated purposes and that some categories of revenue are dedicated to the repayment of such issues.

Nonetheless, fund accounting is insensitive to the joint-product nature of higher education and the fact that the charging of a given activity to a given fund is often a judgment call. The latter is sometimes demonstrated when an administrator, faced with a shortfall in one account, simply off-loads an expenditure or set of expenditures to a different source of funds. As state appropriations have not kept pace with inflation, many institutions have shifted some student affairs costs to the budgets of university centers and residence and dining halls, all self-supporting auxiliary entities. Others have required that faculty members charge more of their own salaries to research grants and contracts. In all of these instances, there is customarily shown some joint product of the activity so that it becomes nearly impossible to determine the extent to which a given project serves general fund, designated, or restricted fund purposes.

The analysis of joint-product activities contained in designated and restricted-fund accounts into a general-use budget is one way to ensure that all sources of revenue are analyzed in preparing a program unit or university's budget for a given year. Elsewhere (Vandament, 1989), I have presented an example of a general use expenditure budget, using a theater department as a case in point. In that example, a basic general fund budget was augmented for general use through the following techniques: (1) Several graduate assistant positions and consumable supplies and equipment used in the instructional program were funded by an excess of revenue over expenditures in performances and workshops conducted by the department. (2) In another instance, the department actually gained general use revenues by making a matching contribution to an endowed chair. In that situation, although the department provided more support for the endowed chair than was funded by the endowment, the investment was considered prudent because the university received more in the value of instruction provided by the occupant of the chair than could have been received with a comparable investment in an adjunct faculty member. (3) Travel funds for professional development, always in short supply in general fund budgets, were provided partially by grant and contract sources.

The variations on such joint-product arrangements are numerous when all of the trade-off possibilities are examined comprehensively and systematically by the administrator planning for the unit. In general, the primary strategies are to engage in activities that produce a profit that can be diverted to general use, and to seek grants and contracts in which the external requirements are a near match for activities that one would legitimately fund from the unrestricted general funds.

Hidden Resources

The accepted method of financial reporting in higher education is based on accrual accounting methods. In accrual accounting, expenditures and income are attributed to the date on which the services were actually completed or the goods were received. The practice of accrual accounting allows one to gain a good index of the net worth of the institution, that is, which assets would be present if the institution closed its doors, canceled outstanding purchase orders, paid the bills for goods and services already received, and collected all revenues for services that had been provided previous to the closure date.

The accrual method avoids many of the pitfalls associated with other accounting methods, for example, recording an expense when a check has been written or recording income when funds have been received and deposited in the institutional bank account. The uneven flow of cash in and out of the university's accounts could give a false impression of its financial health, for example, if it received early payment for services and was late in paying its bills.

At the same time, an exclusive focus on accrual statements can result in at least some neglect of the university's existing assets. Among these assets are the operating funds, usually kept in checking accounts or short-term investments. During periods of high inflation and high interest in the 1970s, many institutions instituted cash management systems to ensure that all funds collected were immediately deposited in interest-bearing accounts, where they remained for as long a time period as possible. These cash management programs placed great strain on the institutions' accountants, who, in past years, had recorded income on the institutions' statements prior to making bank deposits. Now the entries were made after the checks had been deposited. Accounts payable offices were likewise mobilized and devised payment schedules for various vendors based not only on maximizing discounts for early payments but also on making delayed payments to those vendors who would accept late payment without assessing a penalty. In short, the strategy to this day is to keep operating funds under the institution's control in interest-bearing accounts for as long as possible.

As the United States economy shifted to a low inflationary cost and lower interest rates in recent years, cash management programs for operating funds have yielded lower and lower returns. Some aggressive financial managers have moved the cash management activities one step further by analyzing cash flow actually necessary to meet payrolls and pay bills from traditional accounts. Because many institutions have built reserves to cover accrued obligations such as vacation and sick leave, and because the core education programs involve collecting tuition payments early and paying faculty and staff throughout the year, often the available cash in bank accounts and short-term investments exceeds greatly the fund balances that are obtained through accrual accounting methods. For investment purposes, therefore, these managers are converting increasingly more of the operating cash of the institutions into long-term investments, which yield much higher rates of interest or dividends or appreciation. Although there may be some risk to these investments, the diversified portfolios result in risks at an acceptable level and can sometimes double, or perhaps triple, the yield gained from cash management programs.

References

National Association of College and University Business Officers. *Costing for Policy Analysis.* Washington, D.C.: National Association of College and University Business Officers, 1980.

Robinson, D. D., Ray, H. W., and Turk, F. J. "Cost Behavior Analysis for Planning in Higher Education." *NACUBO Professional File,* 1977, 9 (5), 1–51.

Vandament, W. E. *Managing Money in Higher Education: A Guide to the Financial Process and Effective Participation Within It.* San Francisco: Jossey-Bass, 1989.

WILLIAM E. VANDAMENT *is president and professor of psychology at Northern Michigan University, Marquette.*

INDEX

ABC system. *See* Activity-based costing
Activity-based costing: application of, 32–34; development of, 31–32; explanation of, 30; institutional reengineering through, 33
Administrators, 14
American Council on Education, 19
Asset depreciation, 11
Assets: as decision-making framework for budgeting, 12–13; definition of, 9; description of, 9–11; levels of utilization of, 12; methods of acquiring, 12; price of, 12; quality of, 11–12; quantity of, 11; types of, 11
Association of American Colleges, 19

Budgeting, trends in institutional, 35. *See also* Strategic budgeting

Caruthers, K., 5
Coate, L. E., 2
Communication, 41
Cost containment: conclusions regarding, 26; curriculum reform and, 23–26; curriculum structure and, 18–23; general approaches to, 17–18
Costing systems: problems with basic, 30–31; traditional, 31. *See also* Activity-based costing
Cost-revenue relationships, 63–69; fixed and variable costs and, 64–65; hidden resources and, 73–74; high fixed costs and volume and, 66–67; high variable costs and, 67; one-time and recurring considerations and, 69–71; overview of, 63–64; use of all resources and, 71–73; utilization of instructional capacity and, 67–69; volume and revenue generation and, 65
Crosby, P., 43
Curriculum, 10
Curriculum structure: general education and, 18–23; information base for, 23, 25

Decision-making process, 41
Deming, W. E., 43

Endowments, as asset, 10
Enterprise excellence, 29
Equipment, 9

Facilities, 9
Faculty: as asset, 9; early retirement programs for, 38–39; for general education, 25; salary increases for, 6
Financial accounting system, 30
Financial management, 1
Freedman, J. O., 37

General education: institution missions and, 20–21; nature and goals of, 19–20, 26; need for fiscal analysis of, 20; separate faculty for, 25

Hyatt, J. A., 2, 40

Image, as asset, 10
Institutions: budget control systems in, 30; factors of fiscal management in, 63; restructuring by, 35–36; sea change in enterprise behavior by, 29; stages of responses to economic conditions available to, 28
Irvin, G., 25

Jones, D. P., 1
Juran, J. M., 43

Library collections, 9
Lisensky, R. P., 1

McCurdy, L., 37
McMillen, L., 37
Multidimensional analysis: cost-revenue relationships and, 63–69; development of skills in, 63; one-time and recurring considerations and, 69–71

National Association of College and University Business Officers, 1
National Center for Higher Education Management Systems (NCHEMS): cost containment assistance by, 20, 21, 23; costing model established by, 30

Oregon State University: total quality management pilot program at, 43–62. *See also* Total Quality Management pilot program

Orwig, M., 5

Pew Foundation, 26

Reputation, 10
Resources: generation of, 36–38; utilization of, 38–40

Salaries, 6
Santiago, A., 40
Staff, 9. *See also* Faculty
Strategic budgeting: basic concepts of, 8–13; decision-making framework for, 12–13; implications of, 13–15; importance of, 6–7, 15; overview of, 5–6; recommendations regarding, 15–16
Strategic restructuring: explanation of, 36; at University of Maryland, College Park, 36–42
Student body, 9–10

Total Quality Management (TQM): conclusions regarding application of, 61–62; as element of strategic restructuring, 39; preapplication requirements for, 43
Total Quality Management pilot program: budgets and planning team, 50–51; business affairs team A, 52; business affairs team B, 52–53; computing services team, 51–52; conclusions and recommendations regarding, 61–62; creation of, 43–46; customer survey, 55–60; directors' cross-functional team, 60–61; human resources team, 54–55; physical plant team A, 46, 48–49; physical plant team B, 49; printing and mailing team, 49–50; public safety team, 53–54; radiation center team, 54
TQM. *See* Total Quality Management
Turk, F. J., 2

University of California, Voluntary Early Retirement Incentive Program, 38
University of Maryland, College Park: examination of communication at, 41; examination of management processes and procedures in, 39–40; examination of resource utilization at, 38–39; examination of resources and resource generation in, 36–38; strategic restructuring process at, 36, 42
University of Pennsylvania, 19

Vandament, W. E., 2–3

Western Interstate Commission for Higher Education (WICHE), 1
WICHE Watchers, 1
Williamson, O., 38

ORDERING INFORMATION

NEW DIRECTIONS FOR HIGHER EDUCATION is a series of paperback books that provides timely information and authoritative advice about major issues and administrative problems confronting every institution. Books in the series are published quarterly in Spring, Summer, Fall, and Winter and are available for purchase by subscription and individually.

SUBSCRIPTIONS for 1993 cost $47.00 for individuals (a savings of 25 percent over single-copy prices) and $62.00 for institutions, agencies, and libraries. Please do not send institutional checks for personal subscriptions. Standing orders are accepted.

SINGLE COPIES cost $15.95 when payment accompanies order. (California, New Jersey, New York, and Washington, D.C., residents please include appropriate sales tax.) Billed orders will be charged postage and handling.

DISCOUNTS for quantity orders are available. Please write to the address below for information.

ALL ORDERS must include either the name of an individual or an official purchase order number. Please submit your order as follows:
    Subscriptions: specify series and year subscription is to begin
    Single copies: include individual title code (such as HE81)

MAIL ALL ORDERS TO:
    Jossey-Bass Publishers
    350 Sansome Street
    San Francisco, California 94104-1310

FOR SINGLE-COPY SALES OUTSIDE OF THE UNITED STATES CONTACT:
    Maxwell Macmillan International Publishing Group
    866 Third Avenue
    New York, New York 10022-6221

FOR SUBSCRIPTION SALES OUTSIDE OF THE UNITED STATES, contact any international subscription agency or Jossey-Bass directly.

OTHER TITLES AVAILABLE IN THE
NEW DIRECTIONS FOR HIGHER EDUCATION SERIES
Martin Kramer, Editor-in-Chief

HE82   Important Lessons from Innovative Colleges and Universities,
        V. Ray Cardozier
HE81   Recognizing Faculty Work: Reward Systems for the Year 2000,
        Robert M. Diamond, Bronwyn E. Adam
HE80   Assessment and Curriculum Reform, *James L. Ratcliff*
HE79   Agendas for Church-Related Colleges and Universities, *David S. Guthrie,*
        Richard L. Noftzger, Jr.
HE78   Information Literacy: Developing Students as Independent Learners,
        D. W. Farmer, Terrence F. Mech
HE77   The Campus and Environmental Responsibility, *David J. Eagan,*
        David W. Orr
HE76   Administration as a Profession, *Jonathan D. Fife, Lester F. Goodchild*
HE75   Faculty in Governance: The Role of Senates and Joint Committees in
        Academic Decision Making, *Robert Birnbaum*
HE74   The Changing Dimensions of Student Aid, *Jamie P. Merisotis*
HE73   Using Consultants Successfully, *Jon F. Wergin*
HE72   Administrative Careers and the Marketplace, *Kathryn M. Moore*
        Susan B. Twombly
HE71   Managing Change in Higher Education, *Douglas W. Steeples*
HE70   An Agenda for the New Decade, *Larry W. Jones, Franz A. Nowotny*
HE69   Financial Planning Under Economic Uncertainty, *Richard E. Anderson,*
        Joel W. Meyerson
HE67   Achieving Assessment Goals Using Evaluation Techniques, *Peter J. Gray*
HE64   Successful Strategic Planning: Case Studies, *Douglas W. Steeples*
HE63   Research Administration and Technology Transfer, *James T. Kenny*
HE62   Making Computers Work for Administrators, *Kenneth C. Green,*
        Steven W. Gilbert
HE61   Leaders on Leadership: The College Presidency, *James L. Fisher,*
        Martha W. Tack
HE60   Increasing Retention: Academic and Student Affairs Administrators in
        Partnership, *Martha McGinty Stodt, William M. Klepper*
HE59   Student Outcomes Assessment: What Institutions Stand to Gain,
        Diane F. Halpern
HE57   Creating Career Programs in a Liberal Arts Context, *Mary Ann F. Rehnke*
HE52   Making the Budget Process Work, *David J. Berg, Gerald M. Skogley*
HE45   Women in Higher Education Administration, *Adrian Tinsley,*
        Cynthia Secor, Sheila Kaplan